21ST CENTURY READING

CENTURY READING

CREATIVE THINKING AND READING WITH TEDTALKS

Laurie Blass – Mari Vargo – Eunice Yeates – Colleen Sheils

NATIONAL GEOGRAPHIC LEARNING | **CENGAGE Learning**

Australia • Brazil • Japan • Korea • Mexico • Singapore • Spain • United Kingdom • United States

**21st Century Reading Teacher Guide 2
Creative Thinking and Reading with
TED Talks**

Laurie Blass

Mari Vargo

Eunice Yeates

Colleen Sheils

Publisher: Andrew Robinson

Executive Editor: Sean Bermingham

Development Editor: Christopher Street

Editorial Assistant: Dylan Mitchell

Director of Global Marketing: Ian Martin

Product Marketing Manager: Anders Bylund

Media Researcher: Leila Hishmeh

Director of Content and Media Production:
 Michael Burggren

Production Manager: Daisy Sosa

Senior Print Buyer: Mary Beth Hennebury

Cover and Interior Designer:
 Brenda Carmichael

Cover Image: Amy Cuddy: ©James Duncan
 Davidson/TED

Composition: Cenveo® Publisher Services

For permission to use material from this text or product, submit all requests online at **cengage.com/permissions**

Further permissions questions can be emailed to **permissionrequest@cengage.com**

Teacher Guide
ISBN 13: 978-1-305-26632-2

National Geographic Learning/Cengage Learning
20 Channel Center Street
Boston, MA 02210
USA

Cengage Learning is a leading provider of customised learning solutions with office locations around the globe, including Singapore, the United Kingdom, Australia, Mexico, Brazil and Japan. Locate our local office at **international.cengage.com/region**

Cengage Learning products are represented in Canada by Nelson Education Ltd.

Visit National Geographic Learning online at **NGL.Cengage.com**
Visit our corporate website at **www.cengage.com**

Printed in the United States of America
Print Number: 01   Print Year: 2015

CONTENTS

Unit 1
STARTING UP
page 10

Unit 2
FRAGILE FORESTS
page 15

Unit 3
BRIGHT IDEAS
page 20

Unit 4
GAME CHANGERS
page 25

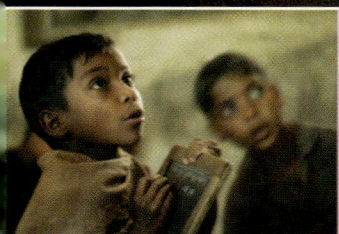

Unit 5
LESSONS IN LEARNING
page 30

Unit 6
FOOD FOR LIFE
page 35

Unit 7
BODY SIGNS
page 40

Unit 8
ENERGY BUILDERS
page 45

Unit 9
CHANGING PERSPECTIVES
page 50

Unit 10
DATA DETECTIVES
page 55

UNIT WALKTHROUGH

21st Century Reading develops core academic language skills and incorporates 21st Century themes and skills such as global awareness, information literacy and critical thinking.

Each unit of the Student Book has three parts:

- **Lesson A:** Students read about a 21st Century topic.
- **Lesson B:** Students view a TED Talk which expands upon the topic in Lesson A.
- **Project:** Students explore the topic further by completing a collaborative research project.

1 Each unit begins with an outline of the learning goals.

2 **Think and Discuss** questions help to raise learners' interest in the unit theme and activate prior knowledge.

Unit 3

A group of women using solar-powered lanterns pick flowers at night in India.

BRIGHT IDEAS

GOALS

IN THIS UNIT, YOU WILL:
- Read about simple inventions that make people's lives better.
- Learn about an invention that is saving babies' lives.
- Explore other simple and creative solutions that improve or save lives.

THINK AND DISCUSS
1. What do you think is the most useful invention ever created? What problem did it solve?
2. What are some big problems that we don't have solutions for yet? Rank them in order of importance.

36 / 37

3 **Lesson A** focuses on a reading passage that provides background and context for the TED Talk in Lesson B.

4 **Pre-reading** activities introduce key terms and content that learners will encounter in the reading passage, and develop previewing skills such as skimming and making predictions.

Lesson A

A Zulu man tries on a pair of adjustable glasses.

PRE-READING

Look at the photos and infographic and read the captions on pages 38–41. Then answer the questions below before discussing with a partner.

Liquid Lenses
1. What do you think their purpose is?
2. How do you think they work?

Fuel Briquettes
1. What do you think their purpose is?
2. Where do you think they are used?
3. Who do you think uses them?

Disaster Shelters
1. What do you think their purpose is?
2. Where do you think they could be used?
3. What problems do you think they solve?

BIG PROBLEMS, SIMPLE SOLUTIONS

Ingenious innovations are improving health and well-being in communities around the world. Speakers at recent TED events have shared simple and inexpensive solutions that can solve everyday problems.

LIQUID LENSES

Many people need eyeglasses, but there often aren't enough eye doctors in the developing world. For example, there's only one optometrist for every 8 million people in some parts of Africa. Physicist Joshua Silver has a solution: **Adjust** your own eyeglasses.

Silver invented eyeglasses that have lenses filled with a liquid. You turn a dial on the sides of the glasses to add or subtract the liquid. Adjusting the amount of liquid changes the strength of the lenses, making it easier for people to see better. The glasses cost $19 today, but Silver hopes to get this down to $1 by 2020.

FUEL BRIQUETTES

In the developing world, smoke from indoor cooking kills more than 2 million children each year. In fact, it's the number one cause of death of children under five. Amy Smith, founder of D-Lab at the Massachusetts Institute of Technology (MIT), discovered a way to make a safe cooking fuel. The material she uses is also free and **plentiful**: farm waste.

Smith invented a low-cost **device** that compresses farm waste into fuel briquettes. These briquettes produce smoke that is less dangerous than the smoke from other fuel, such as wood. They also burn hotter and last longer. Farmers can make these briquettes from readily **available** waste, such as hay in India and corncobs in Ghana. This innovation has an economic benefit, too. Farmers can buy the press for $2 and sell briquettes they don't use. Smith **estimates** that this can increase a farmer's income by $500 a month.

compresses: v. presses together

portable: adj. movable, capable of being carried or moved around

38 / 39

5 Useful academic words and phrases are highlighted in bold and provide the basis for vocabulary building activities later in the lesson.

6 Reading texts are accompanied by glossaries to aid comprehension of lower frequency items that students may be unfamiliar with.

7 **Infographics**, including maps, captions, charts, and graphs, develop learners' visual literacy—their ability to decode graphic information effectively.

8 Reading skill tasks focus on key reading strategies such as identifying main and supporting ideas, and understanding cause/effect relationships.

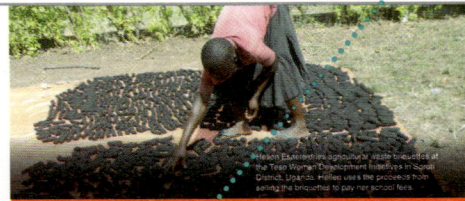

DISASTER SHELTERS

Over 31 million people worldwide lose their homes every year due to natural disasters such as hurricanes and earthquakes. After these disasters, many people live in terrible conditions—in tents or in large arenas with no privacy. Graphic designer Michael McDaniel invented inexpensive, **temporary** housing for people in these situations.

Called the Reaction Exo, these shelters are small, one-room houses that comfortably hold up to four people. They're made from a plastic that is strong, recyclable, and super light. In fact, they're so light that you can lift them by hand. The shelters are very **portable**—you can stack them like paper cups to transport them easily. They snap together, so you can make one large shelter with several rooms. McDaniel hopes that his invention will provide an **affordable** solution to help people rebuild their lives after a natural disaster.

SHIPPING: COMPARISON

20 Reaction Exos
80 People housed
vs.
2 Travel Trailers
8 People housed
vs.
1 Shipping Container
6 People housed

SETUP: 2 MINUTES OR LESS

"Living Room" "Bed Room" "Bath Room"

SAMPLE INDIVIDUAL DEPLOYMENT
(3) Exo upper shells
(2) Exo bases
(1) Exo wet base (integrated plumbing)
(2) doors
(2) connector modules

40

Developing Reading Skills

GETTING THE MAIN IDEAS

A. What do you think the passage is mainly about? Choose the best statement.
   a. Sometimes, common problems can be solved inexpensively.
   b. Advanced technology can help solve some common problems.
   c. Big corporations have solved some common problems.

B. Check (✓) three of the statements below that best describe the benefits of all of the inventions in the passage.
   ____ a. They are inexpensive.
   ____ b. They improve or save lives.
   ____ c. They use local materials.
   ____ d. They are easy to use.

UNDERSTANDING KEY DETAILS
Complete the chart with details about the three inventions described in the passage on pages 38–40.

1. Liquid lenses
2. Farm waste
3. Lightweight and easy to transport
4. Smoke from indoor cooking
5. Amy Smith
6. Liquid
7. Michael McDaniel
8. Plastic
9. Easy to adjust lenses
10. Fuel briquettes
11. Poor shelters for disaster victims
12. Not enough optometrists

Problem	Solution	Inventor	Main Material	Main Benefit
		Joshua Silver		
				Cleaner burning
	Disaster shelters			

41

9 Post-reading tasks incorporate graphic organizers, such as sketch maps, Venn diagrams, and timelines in order to help students visualize and understand key concepts.

10 Vocabulary building tasks focus on the academic words and phrases highlighted in the passage. All target vocabulary is listed at the back of the student book.

11 **Meaning from Context** tasks help learners to understand idiomatic and colloquial expressions.

Developing Reading Skills

UNDERSTANDING VISUALS
Look at the infographic on page 40 and answer the questions.

1. What is the main purpose of the infographic? Check (✓) the two best answers.
   ____ a. To show how quickly an Exo shelter can be set up
   ____ b. To show how much an Exo shelter costs to build
   ____ c. To show how easy it is to transport several Exo shelters

2. How many people can the following types of shelter hold?
   a. 20 Exos: ____
   b. Two travel trailers: ____
   c. One shipping container: ____

3. How long does it take to set up an Exo?

MAKING INFERENCES
Writers sometimes suggest ideas, but they don't state them directly. Readers must infer these ideas.
Check (✓) which of the following statements can be inferred from the passage.

____ 1. An optometrist is a type of doctor who treats eye conditions.
____ 2. Only the richest people in some parts of Africa can be treated by an eye doctor.
____ 3. Joshua Silver feels his eyeglasses will be more successful if they're cheaper.
____ 4. Silver likely got his idea for the eyeglasses while he was a university researcher.
____ 5. Amy Smith hoped to reduce the number of deaths caused by indoor cooking.
____ 6. Wood is a commonly used fuel in developing countries.
____ 7. Smith's fuel briquettes have been most successful so far in India and Ghana.
____ 8. The Exo disaster shelter offers more privacy than other disaster shelters.
____ 9. Michael McDaniel thinks the Exo disaster shelter could also be used as a permanent housing alternative.

42

BUILDING VOCABULARY

A. Complete the sentences with the correct form of the words below.

   adjust   affordable   estimate   plentiful

1. The self-adjusting eyeglasses might cost only $1. This makes them very ____.
2. It's practical to use farm waste to make briquettes because it's very ____. There's a lot of it everywhere in the world.
3. People can ____ the lenses of Silver's eyeglasses by themselves.
4. Smith isn't sure how much money farmers can make by selling the fuel briquettes, but she ____ that it might be around $500 a month.

B. Complete each statement with the correct word.

1. If something is **temporary**, it is there for a ____ amount of time.
   a. long   b. short
2. If something is **available**, it's ____ to get.
   a. hard   b. easy
3. Another word for **device** is "____."
   a. idea   b. equipment
4. If something is **portable**, it is ____ to carry around.
   a. easy   b. hard

GETTING MEANING FROM CONTEXT

A. Find the phrase "get this down to" in paragraph 2. What do you think it means?
   a. to lower an amount   b. to sell something in more places   c. to make something shorter

B. The passage mentions that the fuel briquettes have an "economic benefit". What does this phrase mean? Discuss with a partner.

CRITICAL THINKING
Evaluating Which of the three inventions do you think could be the most useful for your country? Why?

EXPLORE MORE
Learn more about Silver's, Smith's, and McDaniel's inventions by watching their TED Talks at TED.com. Find out more places where people are using these innovations. Share your information with the class.

43

12 **Critical Thinking** questions encourage students to analyze, evaluate, and apply ideas to their own experience, as well as synthesizing ideas from the reading and the talk.

13 **Explore More** sections provide suggestions for further reading or viewing – such as related TED Talks and National Geographic articles.

14 **Lesson B** focuses on the key ideas in a TED Talk that relates to the overall unit theme.

> Lesson B
>
> **TED**TALKS
>
> # A WARM EMBRACE THAT SAVES LIVES
>
> **JANE CHEN** Social Entrepreneur, TED speaker
>
> In 2008, Jane Chen went to India with the goal of solving a terrible problem: infant mortality. More than a quarter of infant deaths in the world occur in India, and many of these deaths occur because a baby is born premature.
>
> Premature babies can't regulate their own body temperatures because they don't have enough fat to stay warm. Because they can't keep warm, the babies are not able to grow properly. Those babies that do survive sometimes grow up with long-term health problems such as diabetes or heart disease.
>
> Many of these problems could be prevented if premature babies were kept warm. Chen spent time talking to mothers and health workers in India. She quickly realized that expensive, high-tech solutions—such as incubators—were not the answer. As Chen says, she wanted to help people by creating a more "human-centered design."
>
> **mortality:** n. the rate of death from illness
> **premature:** adj. born too early
> **regulate:** v. control
> **incubator:** n. a special hospital bed with a cover, used to warm babies
>
> In this lesson, you are going to watch Chen's TED Talk. Use the information about Chen above to answer the questions.
>
> 1. What health problem did Jane Chen study in India?
>
> 2. Why do premature babies sometimes develop health issues later in life?
>
> 3. Why do you think an expensive, high-tech solution is not the answer in India?
>
> Chen's idea worth spreading is that we can save babies' lives, and improve their quality of life in the long term, with a simple, low-cost infant warmer.
>
> 44 / 45

15 A short reading passage provides background information about the speaker.

16 Comprehension questions check students' understanding of the speaker's background.

17 A previewing task typically features a short excerpt from the TED Talk together with questions helping students to predict the main theme.

> **TED**TALKS
>
> **PART 1**
>
> ## A BIG PROBLEM
>
> ### PREVIEWING
>
> Complete the excerpt from Chen's talk with the words below.
>
> | electricity | hot-water bottles | light bulbs | rural | unsafe |
>
> . . . [T]raditional incubators require _____ and cost up to $20,000. So, you're not going to find them in _____ areas of developing countries. As a result, parents resort to local solutions like tying _____ around their babies' bodies, or placing them under _____—methods that are both ineffective and _____.
>
> **resort to:** v. do something extreme because of limited choices
>
> ### IDENTIFYING SOLUTIONS
>
> **A.** Watch the first segment of Chen's TED Talk and check your answers to the Previewing activity. Then answer the question below.
>
> What two solutions have local people tried in the past? Why do you think these solutions work? Discuss with a partner.
>
> **B.** Read the excerpt below. Then choose the three best features for a local solution to the problem.
>
> [M]y team and I realized what was needed was a local solution, something that could work without electricity, that was simple enough for a mother or a midwife to use, given that the majority of births still take place in the home. We needed something that was portable, something that could be sterilized and reused across multiple babies, and something ultra low-cost . . .
>
> **midwife:** n. a person whose job is to help women when they are giving birth
> **sterilized:** v. to make completely free of dirt and germs
>
> Chen realized the solution to the problem should be _____, _____, and _____.
>
> 1. powered with electricity
> 2. easy to move around
> 3. affordable
> 4. attractively designed
> 5. made from recycled materials
> 6. easy to clean
>
> **CRITICAL THINKING**
>
> 1. **Synthesizing.** How are the problems Chen describes similar to the ones described in the passage in Lesson A?
>
> 2. **Predicting.** How do you think Chen solved the problem of keeping premature babies warm?
>
> **PART 2**
>
> ## A BETTER SOLUTION
>
> ### UNDERSTANDING DETAILS
>
> Read the following excerpt from Chen's talk and answer the questions (1–3). Then watch this segment of her talk to check your answers.
>
> What you see here looks nothing like an incubator. It looks like a small sleeping bag for a baby. You can open it up completely. It's waterproof. There's no seams inside so you can sterilize it very easily. But the magic is in this pouch of wax. This is a phase-change material. It's a wax-like substance with a melting point of human body temperature, 37 degrees Celsius. You can melt this simply using hot water and then when it melts it's able to maintain one constant temperature for four to six hours at a time, after which you simply reheat the pouch. So, you then place it into this little pocket back here, and it creates a warm micro-environment for the baby.
>
> Looks simple, but we've reiterated this dozens of times by going into the field to talk to doctors, moms, and clinicians to ensure that this really meets the needs of the local communities.
>
> **seams:** n. lines where two pieces of cloth are sewed together
> **phase-change material:** adj. a substance that changes in some way; for example, from a solid to a liquid
>
> 1. What is the phase-change material?
>   a. Something like water
>   b. Something like wax
>
> 2. What happens when the phase-change material melts?
>   a. It gets to the same temperature as the human body.
>   b. It sterilizes the pouch.
>
> 3. Why is this phase-change material useful for Chen's invention?
>
> 46 / 47

18 Guided comprehension tasks focus on the speaker's main ideas, and language he/she uses to convey those ideas.

19 The adapted TED Talks are often divided into two or three parts, each with associated activities. These parts are also noted in the video transcripts at the back of the Student Book.

20 A range of visuals are incorporated to summarize key points of the talk and also to preview subject-specific terminology.

21 Each unit concludes with a project-based activity which brings together ideas from the unit in a productive task.

22 **Projects** take the form of research assignments, short presentations, interviews etc. The Teacher's Guide provides advice for teachers in terms of structuring the project and also suggests functional language to pre-teach before students begin the task.

Series Components

An **Audio CD** features narrations of each reading passage and TED speaker profile. These are highlighted by a (🎧) icon in the Student Book.

A **DVD** accompanying the series contains each adapted TED Talk. Each talk can also be viewed online (visit NGL.Cengage.com/21centuryreading). Viewing activities are highlighted by a (▶) icon in the Student Book.

A photocopiable **TED Talk Summary Worksheet** is provided on page 9 of this Teacher's Guide. This can be used to aid students' comprehension of the TED Talks featured in the Student Book, or those recommended as extension activities.

Annotated Video Transcripts for each TED Talk can be found on pages 60–79 of this Teacher's Guide. These provide explanations of language items and cultural references that may be unfamiliar to students.

Other components in the series include:

- an interactive **Student eBook**
- an interactive **Instructor eBook** that can be used as a presentation tool in class
- an **Assessment CD-ROM** containing ExamView® question banks for teachers who want to create customized tests or give students additional language practice.

WELCOME TO 21ST CENTURY READING!

Globalization and the internet are changing the way students learn. Today's young adult and adult ESL/EFL learners need to develop not only core academic English skills such as reading, viewing, and vocabulary skills, but also essential global and cross-cultural awareness, creative and critical thinking skills, and information and media literacies.

In **21st Century Reading**, motivating speakers and innovative content from TED—and its focus on **ideas worth spreading**—provide an exciting opportunity to inspire learners as they develop these essential skills.

The main objective of **21st Century Reading** is to enable learners to understand and respond to ideas and content in English, by reading articles adapted for level and viewing related TED talks. The focus is on the key ideas of each text and talk—and the language that the writer or speaker uses to convey those ideas. In most cases, the TED Talk has been abridged to focus on two or three segments that best represent the speaker's key ideas.

As learners progress through the series, they develop essential reading and vocabulary skills, such as scanning quickly for specific information, making connections between main and supporting ideas, and inferring meaning from context. In addition, learners are encouraged to think critically about each text and TED talk, for example by:

- **Analyzing** an article or excerpt in detail in order to identify key points and arguments.
- **Evaluating** evidence to decide how credible, relevant, or sufficient the information is.
- **Reasoning** and justifying solutions to a problem, based on logical conclusions.
- **Inferring** what a writer or speaker is saying indirectly, and interpreting figurative language.
- **Synthesizing** ideas from more than one source in order to make a judgment or conclusion.
- **Predicting** what will happen, either later in the text or at a future time.
- **Reflecting** on a writer's/speaker's ideas and applying those ideas to other contexts.

We hope that you—and your students—enjoy your journey through **21st Century Reading**, and that along the way you discover many ideas worth spreading!

Name: _____   Class: _____

TED Talk Summary Worksheet

Unit: _____   Video Title: _____

Speaker: _____

What information do you learn about the speaker and their background?

_____

_____

_____

Summarize the main idea of the talk in one sentence.

_____

What supporting details or examples does the speaker use to support their idea?

_____

_____

_____

How does the speaker engage the audience? For example, using images, charts, humor, actions.

_____

_____

_____

What is your opinion of the talk? What words or phrases would you use to describe it?

_____

_____

_____

What language in the video was new to you? Make a note of three words or phrases that the speaker used. Write a sentence or definition for each one.

_____

_____

_____

STARTING UP

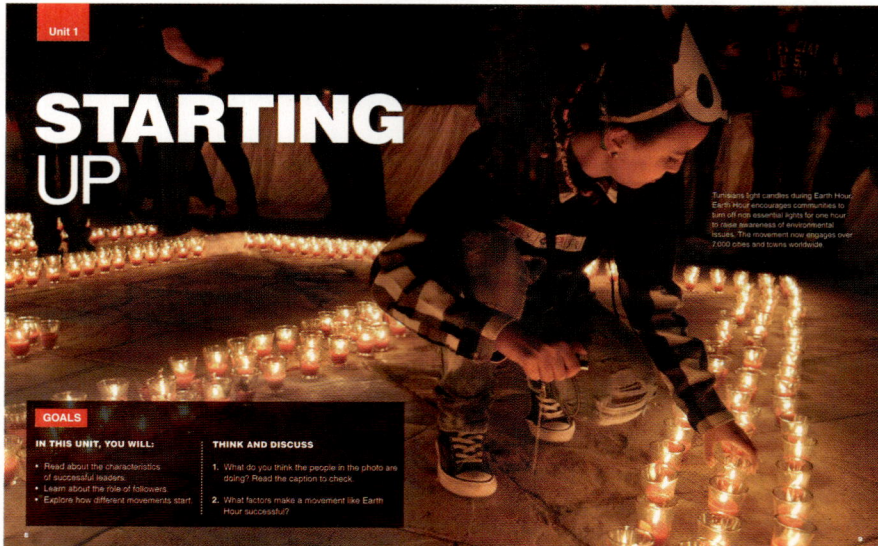

UNIT OVERVIEW

Reading: Students read about how successful leaders inspire others to follow them.

TED Talk: Entrepreneur Derek Sivers shows a video of a movement being born and discusses exactly how it happens.

Project: Students research a movement and present on why it became popular.

Lesson 1A INSPIRED LEADERSHIP

LESSON OVERVIEW

Aims

- Read and comprehend an article about inspirational leaders and how and why people want to follow them.
- Identify main and supporting ideas.
- Understand references.

Target Vocabulary: attract, features, focus, in other words, leadership, purpose, show up, stand out

Reading Passage Summary: Students read about ideas on leadership developed by Simon Sinek, an author who studies how and why leaders inspire people to follow them. He says that great leaders have a focus and a clear purpose and can communicate them to others. Once people understand clearly what a leader believes, they can make a decision to join that leader. Sinek points out that followers are not unthinking. When we share the same beliefs, it becomes our choice to follow a leader. The same applies for organizations and companies that we choose to patronize.

TEACHING NOTES

THINK AND DISCUSS

The unit deals with the theme of leaders and followers. Go over the goals of the unit and elicit the meaning of *movement*. Make sure students understand that it refers to a situation where a large group of people try to affect change, usually of a social or political nature. For question 2, elicit ideas from students of what inspires people to join certain movements. Earth Hour started in 2007 in Sydney, Australia, to raise awareness about environmental issues and is now an annual event in countries all over the world. Students can find out more about Earth Hour at earthhour.com.

PRE-READING

A. Elicit or explain the meaning of *inspiring*. Give students a minute or so to think about and write their answers before discussing with a partner. Ask pairs to share with the class one quality of a successful leader. Draw a mind map on the board of students' ideas. Use the map to aid discussions throughout the lesson.

Think and Discuss

1. They are lighting candles for Earth Hour, an event that encourages people to conserve electricity.
2. Answers will vary. A movement is usually considered successful if it becomes popular, and it is generally spread by members who believe in it and work hard to make it well known.

Pre-reading

A. Answers will vary. Possible qualities include: strength, commitment, dedication, purpose, belief, sense of justice, communication skills, public appeal, likeability, etc.

B. Answers will vary.

C. Predictions will vary. The passage is about how leaders inspire us.

Getting the Main Ideas

1. what they believe; **2.** It is important for followers to share the same beliefs as leaders.

Identifying Supporting Ideas

A. The following words should be underlined: **Paragraph 2:** For example; **Paragraph 3:** To illustrate this; **Paragraph 4:** for instance.

B. **1.** b; **2.** c; **3.** a

C. **1.** SI; **2.** MI; **3.** SI; **4.** SI; **5.** SI

Understanding References

1. great leaders; **2.** King's followers; **3.** Apple's followers; **4.** people who lead/people we follow

Building Vocabulary

A. **1.** showed up; **2.** in other words; **3.** focus; **4.** attract

B. **1.** c; **2.** a; **3.** d; **4.** b

Getting Meaning from Context

To be "easily led" means that you are quick to follow others, suggesting that you lack independent thought.

Critical Thinking

1. Answers will vary; **2.** Answers will vary. Possibilities include: TV stars, musicians, editors of popular online websites, bloggers.

B. Elicit the meaning of *civil rights leader* or explain more about Martin Luther King Jr. Students should recognize that he was a key figure in fighting racial and social inequality in the United States in the 1960s. Have students discuss how he was able to create such a huge network of support, which led to major changes in the United States. Point out, as the first paragraph of the reading does, that this was before technology made creating support networks easier. *Extension:* Have students search online to learn more about Martin Luther King Jr. Ask them to write down the various adjectives they see used to describe King. Have them share them with the class. Note if any of them match qualities on the mind map on the board from Exercise A.

C. Have students work individually to complete Exercise C before checking their answers in pairs.

DEVELOPING READING SKILLS

GETTING THE MAIN IDEAS

Have students read the entire passage, either silently or while listening to the narrated passage on the audio. Have them answer the questions individually before checking in pairs. For question 2, ask students if they agree with what the author says about followers.

IDENTIFYING SUPPORTING IDEAS

A. Review the meaning of *supporting details*. Make sure students understand that they support the topic sentence, or main idea, of a paragraph. Note that there are three phrases that students will find in the passage for introducing supporting details.

B. Have students work individually to complete the activity. Check answers together, eliciting the main idea for each supporting idea.

C. Ensure students underline and focus on the full sentence in the passage. For the supporting details, elicit the main ideas that they support.

UNDERSTANDING REFERENCES

Review the meaning of *reference*. Note that some students may be more familiar with the term *pronoun reference*. Have students work individually to complete the activity. Check answers as a class. Explain that references are used by writers to give variety to sentences in order to avoid repetition.

BUILDING VOCABULARY

A. Have students complete Exercise A individually before checking answers as a class. Make sure students recognize the difference between *standing out* due to being unique or better and *standing outside*.

B. Have students complete Exercise B individually before checking answers as a class. **Extension:** Have students work individually to write new sentences about leadership using the target vocabulary.

GETTING MEANING FROM CONTEXT

Give students a minute to write their answers. To be "easily led" means that you are quick to follow others, suggesting that you lack independent thought. **Extension:** Ask students to think about a time when they were easily led and why. Have them share this experience with a partner.

CRITICAL THINKING

Give students a minute to think about their answers before sharing with a partner. For question 1, encourage students to think about well-known leaders and not so well-known ones. For example, it may be a family member, teacher, or sports coach. For question 2, go back to the mind map on the board. Elicit a discussion about important leadership qualities in various areas of life. **Extension:** Have students share with a partner a time when they had the chance to be a leader.

EXPLORE MORE

Have students watch Sinek's TED Talk while completing a TED Talk summary worksheet (see page 9 of this Teacher's Guide). He says that what makes successful people and organizations different from others is that they work from the inside out. By this, he means that they know their purpose, cause, and belief first, and communicate it successfully, which is why people follow them.

Lesson 1B | HOW TO START A MOVEMENT

LESSON OVERVIEW

Aims:
- Watch and understand a talk that highlights the stages of a new movement.
- Recognize main ideas.
- Identify tone and attitude.

TED Talk Summary: In his playful TED Talk, Derek Sivers shows a three-minute video that starts with one man dancing alone and ends with a crowd dancing alongside him. Sivers dissects this scene to talk about how a movement is made. He outlines each stage of the movement and then talks about lessons we learn from understanding these stages, namely the initial gutsiness of the leader and the very critical role of the first follower, who actually is the one who gathers all the others. An annotated transcript for the edited TED Talk is on pages 60–61 of this Teacher's Guide.

TEACHING NOTES

The passage introduces the speaker and some unusual choices he has made in work and life. Have students read the passage, either silently or while listening to the narrated passage on the audio, before answering the comprehension questions. When checking answers, elicit students' predictions for question 3, and write their ideas on the board.

PART 1

PREVIEWING

A. Have students complete Exercise A individually before checking answers in pairs.

B. Give students time to work individually to look over the synonyms and read the excerpt. Encourage students to try substituting the synonyms for the terms in order to guess their meanings. Have students check their answers to A and B as they watch the video. Note that Sivers says, "Now we've got a movement," as a big group joins the first three dancers. After that, a lot of people still continue to join the crowd, which is why item a is the final one in the sequence. While Sivers says, "And that's how you make a movement," right after the final group of people join the dancers, he has already pinpointed the exact moment when the movement happened, which is before the last members run to join. Finally, go over each of the terms and its meaning for Exercise B.

1. CD Baby was a company started by Derek Sivers to sell independent music online; 2. The lessons he learned from starting, managing, and selling a business; 3. Guesses will vary. The people are dancing and getting others to join, illustrating the stages of starting a movement.

PART 1

Previewing

A. Guesses will vary. Actual answers are: **a.** 6; **b.** 2; **c.** 5; **d.** 4; **e.** 1; **f.** 3

B. a. 4; **b.** 3; **c.** 2; **d.** 1; **e.** 5

Getting the Main Ideas

A. 1. T; **2.** F; **3.** T

B. Those who don't join might be ridiculed.

Critical Thinking

Answers will vary.

PART 2

Previewing

The following should be underlined: the shirtless guy who was first

Recognizing Main Ideas

A. c

B. Students' points on the chart will vary. General answers are: **1.** red area; **2.** red area; **3.** yellow-orange area; **4.** blue area; **5.** yellow-orange area

Getting Meaning from Context

People who are "sitting on the fence" are undecided about whether to join or not. "The tipping point" refers to the moment that a new movement or trend becomes popular.

Identifying Tone and Attitude

Sivers uses a humorous tone to communicate his ideas about how movements are made.

Critical Thinking

Both Sivers and Sinek talk about the importance of the role of followers. Both point out that followers are making their own choices when joining a leader. Sinek talks about how followers must already share the same beliefs as their leader while Sivers explains that followers, especially the early ones, might actually do more to lead the movement than the leader.

GETTING THE MAIN IDEAS

A. Have students work individually to answer the questions before checking their answers in pairs.

B. Have students discuss their answers in pairs. Sivers notes that the individuals who join at the very end are the ones who are afraid of being left out and ridiculed.

CRITICAL THINKING

Give students a minute to think about their answers before discussing in pairs. Ask students to give reasons why they might be a leader or follower in this movement.

PART 2

PREVIEWING

Before students read the excerpt, elicit the meaning of "get the credit" and "over-glorified." Then ask pairs to discuss the meaning of the quote.

RECOGNIZING MAIN IDEAS

A. Play the video. Then have students complete Exercise A. Check answers as a class. Ask students to summarize what Sivers says about leaders and followers.

B. Give students time to look over the chart showing level of risk before having them work individually to complete it. Note that the points on the chart that students mark may vary, but they should have the general area correct.

GETTING MEANING FROM CONTEXT

Have students work individually to write their answers before checking with a partner. Point out the visual image in the phrase "sitting on the fence." A person sitting on a fence is between two places. The term is used to describe when you haven't yet made up your mind about something.

IDENTIFYING TONE AND ATTITUDE

Have students complete the activity individually before checking answers as a class. In addition to Sivers's tone in his speech, we can see the humor by his choice of video as well as by the lively response and laughter from the audience.

CRITICAL THINKING

Have students discuss in pairs. Ask them to write some quick notes on what Sivers thinks first, and then check the article in Lesson A to write down Sinek's main points. Ask students to think about what people who want to be leaders can learn from what both men say, and to think about what lessons they personally can take away from the article and the TED Talk.

EXPLORE MORE

Have students watch Sivers's other TED Talk at Ted.com while completing a TED Talk summary worksheet (see page 9 of this Teacher's Guide). A social reality is when the mind is tricked into believing a goal is already accomplished before it actually is, which is what Sivers says happens when we tell others about our goals before working on them.

Project # RESEARCHING OTHER MOVEMENTS

PROJECT OVERVIEW:

Aims
- Students work in pairs to research a movement and find out how it was created.
- Students use what they learned in the TED Talk to present on the stages of the movement.
- Students compare and discuss the movements that were researched.

Summary: Students research a movement and try to find out why and how it became so popular. Students make a time line to trace the movement's origins, and present about the movement to another pair.

Materials: computer, access to the Internet, presentation software

Language Support: Telling a story: *It all started when . . .; Suddenly . . .; On that day . . .*

TEACHING NOTES

PREPARATION

Have students work in pairs. Tell them to look over the list of movements. Give them a few minutes to discuss movements they know and decide which one to research. Check each pair's choice to ensure that a variety of movements are being researched and presented on. If necessary, go over the list of research questions as a class. Point out that it is OK for students to choose a movement that is no longer popular. Note the "Language Support" phrases above on the board, and review them before students begin the activity.

DURING THE PROJECT

Monitor as pairs work together and give assistance or feedback when necessary as they prepare their presentations. Point out that students should especially look at leaders and followers, as well as try to find the tipping point in the movement. If necessary, write a sample time line on the board using the movement in Sivers's TED Talk. If time permits, encourage students to find pictures online to use during their presentations. Give pairs a few minutes to practice their presentations. Then have pairs present to two other pairs.

AFTER THE PROJECT

Asks students to review the questions in B before they listen to the presentations. Point out that they should be taking notes as they listen, with the goal of comparing the movements. After all pairs have presented, have groups discuss and compare. Ask students to share with the class which movement they would become a follower of and why.

EXPLORE MORE

Have students work in pairs to go to TED's site and check the list of talks on leadership before choosing one and watching. Have students complete a TED Talk summary worksheet (see page 9 of this Teacher's Guide). Ask pairs to share what they learned.

FRAGILE FORESTS

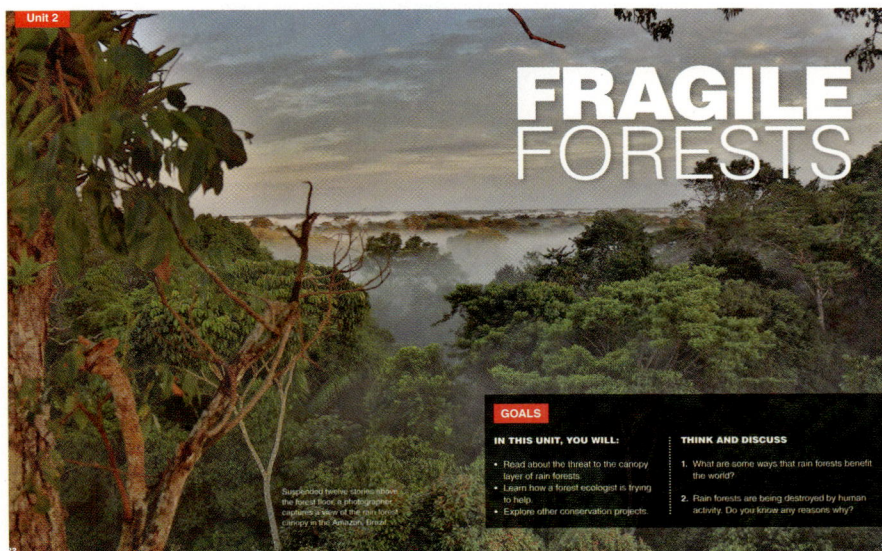

UNIT OVERVIEW

Reading: Students learn about the importance of epiphytes in the rain forests and scientist Nalini Nadkarni's work to conserve the endangered plant life.

TED Talk: Nadkarni talks about outreach programs she's created to help save the rain forest canopy.

Project: Students research and talk about a community outreach program.

Lesson 2A TROUBLE FOR THE AIR PLANTS

LESSON OVERVIEW

Aims:
- Read and comprehend an article about the important role epiphytes play in the rain forest.
- Understand key details and meaning from context.
- Scan for information.

Target Vocabulary: attach, capacity, damaged, innovative, layer, mysterious, survive, sustainable

Reading Passage Summary: Students read about the rain forest canopy and especially the epiphyte plants, or mosses, that grow there. These plants survive by getting nutrients and water from the air. Since balance of light, nutrients, and water in the rain forest has been disrupted by human activity, the epiphytes are now in trouble. In other parts of the world, epiphytes are taken off trees and sold, even though it takes over 20 years for them to grow back. To educate the public about the critical role that epiphytes play in the health of the rain forest and the world in general, scientist Nalini Nadkarni is working hard to create outreach programs.

TEACHING NOTES

THINK AND DISCUSS

This unit introduces problems threatening forests, especially rain forests. As a whole-class activity, ask students to talk about what they know about rain forests and what makes them important for the world. Rain forests are home to an extraordinary number of plants and wildlife—about 50 percent of the world's animal species and two-thirds of plant species live in the rain forest. The plants there take in carbon dioxide and help keep the Earth's air clean. The rain forests also keep and store rainwater for the planet. Additionally, many medicinal plants and herbs can be found in the rain forests. Elicit ideas on how the rain forests are being destroyed. Human activity affecting the rain forests includes cattle ranching, logging, development, and agriculture, among others.
Extension: Have students work in pairs to search online for more information (not mentioned in the brainstorm about rain forests) about the importance of rain forests and what's destroying them. Then have them teach the class what they learned.

Think and Discuss

A. Answers will vary. Possibilities include:
1. Rain forests provide a home for a majority of the world's plants and animals. The plants there absorb a lot of the world's carbon dioxide; **2.** logging, development, agriculture, ranching, etc.

Pre-reading

A. 1. The top layer has high temperatures and wind. Plant life is limited. The bottom layer also has limited plant life, but because it is dark; **2.** The canopy has the easiest living conditions, including plentiful sunlight and shelter from the wind.

B. Answers will vary. She is climbing to the top of a tree to view (and study) the rain forest canopy.

C. Answers will vary, however students should recognize the reading is on the destruction of the rain forests.

Getting the Main Ideas

The following should be checked: 2, 4.

Understanding Key Details

1. forests; **2.** mosses; **3.** canopy; **4.** roots, host; **5.** nutrients, water; **6.** slowly

Scanning for Information

1. 28,000; **2.** 100 feet/30 meters; **3.** over 20 years

Building Vocabulary

A. 1. a, c, d; **2.** a, b, d; **3.** b, c, d; **4.** d

B. mysterious; layers; damage; survive

Understanding Meaning from Context

1. b; **2.** b

Critical Thinking

1. Answers will vary. Possibilities include: writing about it, taking pictures of it, teaching people directly, etc.

2. Answer will vary. Nadkarni wants people to feel connected to the trees so they care about them. She believes that if people care about the trees, they will help to save them.

PRE-READING

A. Give students a few minutes to look at the pictures and read the information in the diagram on page 26 before sharing answers in pairs.

B. Tell students to look at the picture and make guesses with a partner before reading the caption to check their answers. Nadkarni is a tree scientist, forest ecologist, and conservationist. Ask them to guess what other means she uses to get up to the canopy.

C. Make sure students have access to a dictionary. Give students a couple of minutes to scan the words and look up the ones they don't know. Then have them discuss their ideas in pairs. Elicit the meaning of each term and students' guesses about the passage topic.

DEVELOPING READING SKILLS

GETTING THE MAIN IDEAS

Have students read the entire passage, either silently or while listening to the narrated passage on the audio. Have them identify the main problems individually before checking answers in pairs.

UNDERSTANDING KEY DETAILS

Remind students that supporting details are what an author uses to communicate the main message or idea of a piece of writing. In this case, the key details about epiphytes tell us why it is necessary that we protect them. Have students complete the sentences individually before checking as a class.

SCANNING FOR INFORMATION

Go over the information about when and how to scan. Make sure students understand that we scan for specific information. Tell students that when scanning for the answers, which are all numerical, they should read very quickly to find numbers with the appropriate units. For example, a question about length of time might be answered in years, hours, minutes, etc.

BUILDING VOCABULARY

A. Have students complete Exercise A individually before checking answers as a class. Something that is *innovative* introduces a unique way of doing something. It is often used to describe a new invention, product, or idea that changes the way we do something. The adjective *sustainable* has become an important term in environmental science, used to describe something that does not deplete natural resources.

B. Have students complete Exercise B individually before checking answers as a class. Note that students will see video of Nadkarni climbing a giant strangler fig in Lesson B during her TED Talk.

UNDERSTANDING MEANING FROM CONTEXT

Explain that understanding meaning from context in this case involves looking at what the author is saying in the sentence as well as the words used. Have students complete questions 1 and 2 individually before checking answers as a class. When you *capture someone's attention*, you do something that catches their interest and makes them listen. The term *spread the word* is commonly used to talk about sharing information with many people.

CRITICAL THINKING

Have students discuss in pairs before having the class brainstorm some ideas for capturing people's attention and spreading the word about rain forests. Encourage students to think about ways to use popular culture and technology to engage a young audience. Nadkarni talks about how many people live in cities today and therefore lack a strong connection to nature because there are not a lot of trees around them. Make sure students understand that she thinks this lack of a connection with nature means that we don't care as much as we should about saving the trees and the rain forests.

EXPLORE MORE

On National Geographic's rain forest page, students can learn more about the habitat, reasons for deforestation, and ways people are working to help save rain forests.

Lesson 2B CONSERVING THE CANOPY

LESSON OVERVIEW

Aims:
- Watch and understand a talk about ways to help conserve the rain forest.
- Understand the main idea.
- Recognize purpose and supporting evidence.

TED Talk Summary: In her TED Talk, forest ecologist Nalini Nadkarni talks about her connection to trees and why she believes that restoring this connection for others will help save the rain forests. She shows us the damage happening to the rain forest due to deforestation, and talks about how scientists need to learn to work with the public to save the forests. She then describes a program she started where prisoners grow moss, which is helping to save the forests in the Pacific Northwest. An annotated transcript for the edited TED Talk is on pages 62–63 of this Teacher's Guide.

TEACHING NOTES

The paragraph and questions talk more about some of the collaborative efforts Nadkarni has begun to get the general public more interested in saving the rain forests. She has worked with dance choreographers and rap artists, and she also created a program to bring

schoolchildren from poorer city neighborhoods to experience the rain forest. Because Nadkarni's interest in trees began when she was a child, she believes that if people in cities, children especially, have more direct contact with trees, they'll care more about saving them. ***Extension:*** Have students search online to find and watch Lomask's Biome dance.

PART 1

PREVIEWING

A. Have students work individually to write their ideas before sharing them with a partner. Remind students of the diagram on page 26 that they studied in Lesson A. This should give them some ideas of what Nadkarni sees as she climbs through the layers of the rain forest to the canopy.

RECOGNIZING PURPOSE

A. Play the video. Have students check their answers to Previewing as they watch.

B. Have students work individually to answer before checking answers as a class. Option a is the best answer. Nadkarni is highlighting the beauty of the canopy in order to encourage people to help save it.

1. Nadkarni's interest in trees began when she was a child, and she climbed them for fun.

2. She was inspired by a trip with Nadkarni to the Costa Rican rain forest.

3. middle-school children from the inner-city

PART 1

Previewing

Guesses will vary. She sees various wildlife and plant life, as well as the views of forest and deforestation around her.

Recognizing Purpose

B. a

C. a, b

Critical Thinking

Answers will vary. Both the height and size of the canopy likely present issues for the camera crew and filmmakers.

PART 2

Previewing

A. Guesses will vary. Nadkarni talks about how she's created a program with prisons to have inmates grow mosses.

B. 1. grow; **2.** help; **3.** nature; **4.** time

Understanding the Main Ideas

B. The following should be underlined: organic gardens, worm cultures, recycling, water catchment, beekeeping.

C. 3

Recognizing Supporting Evidence

A. 1. statistic **2.** comparison **3.** example

B. The following should be underlined: **1.** 265-million-dollar industry; **2.** is a lot more than; **3.** organic gardens, worm cultures, recycling, water catchment, beekeeping

Critical Thinking

1. Answers will vary. The wardens probably like the project because it gives the prisoners a chance to do meaningful work and have a positive influence on society.

2. Answers will vary. Nadkarni is not the first ecologist to focus on the rain forests, but her movement is specifically about saving the rain forest canopies. Her followers are likely people who feel a connection with and care about trees and the future of our planet's forests.

Explore More

Nadkarni also talks about a program to save tree frogs in the Pacific Northwest in the United States.

C. Have students check their answers in pairs. Note that the information students learned in Lesson A, about Nadkarni's desire to save the epiphytes, should help them narrow their answer choices here.

CRITICAL THINKING

Give students a few minutes to discuss their ideas with a partner. Then have a class discussion to brainstorm some ideas about how the film crew was able to take video of the canopy.

PART 2

PREVIEWING

A. Give students time to go back to Lesson A and briefly review what they learned about epiphytes. Point out that they've already learned about some outreach programs

that Nadkarni has started in the introduction to Lesson B. Ask them to discuss and brainstorm some other possible outreach programs together.

B. Have students work individually to complete the paragraph before comparing answers in pairs. Then have students summarize the meaning of the paragraph.

UNDERSTANDING THE MAIN IDEAS

A. Play the TED Talk. Then check answers to Previewing as a class. Ask students to identify who is helping Nadkarni grow mosses (men and women in prison). Then elicit the reasons (listed in the paragraph in Previewing) why she chose prisoners for this project.

B. Give students a minute to work individually to scan the paragraph and underline the projects before checking answers as a class.

C. Have students work individually to answer the question before checking answers as a class. Note that while Nadkarni talks a lot about having the prisoners help grow moss, the main point of this part of her talk is to discuss how scientists can create outreach programs.

RECOGNIZING SUPPORTING EVIDENCE

A. Have students read the sentence on supporting evidence. Then elicit the role of supporting evidence. Make sure students understand that in writing, examples, statistics, and comparisons support the main idea, or topic sentence, of a paragraph. In speaking, they serve the same purpose, to support the point of the speaker.

B. Have students work individually before comparing answers with a partner. Remind students to use their scanning skills to find the information quickly.

CRITICAL THINKING

Give students time to think about their answer to the question first before sharing their thoughts in pairs. Then open up a discussion about question 2 to the class, encouraging students to give opinions and reasons to support their opinions.

EXPLORE MORE

In Nadkarni's complete TED Talk, she talks about more outreach programs and shows video of some of the programs students read about in Lesson A.

Project — RESEARCHING A SUSTAINABILITY PROJECT

PROJECT OVERVIEW:

Aims
- Students research in pairs about a sustainability project and then present to others.
- Students practice giving a formalized and persuasive report.
- Students listen to each other's reports and decide which project to support.

Summary: Students research a sustainability project and produce a report to inspire their classmates to join.

Materials: computer, Internet access, presentation software

Language Support: Presentation language: *Today I am going to introduce* . . . ; *Let me first explain* . . . ; *Let's next talk about* . . .

TEACHING NOTES

PREPARATION

Have students work in pairs. Ask them to find a sustainability project or program that focuses on either a global cause, such as saving the rain forest canopies, or a more local one, such as saving moss in the Pacific Northwest. Make sure they know that a local cause should be something from their own area or the area near their school. Tell them to research as much as they can about both the project and the initiative it supports. Encourage them to use the questions on page 35 as a guide in their research. Note the

"Language Support" phrases above on the board and review them before students begin the activity.

DURING THE PROJECT

After pairs choose and research their projects and initiatives, give them time to create their reports. Point out that they should have pictures and/or video to support their presentations, like Nadkarni did. Remind them that their goal is to persuade others to support the program, so they must make their talk engaging and persuasive. Monitor as pairs prepare their presentations, and give assistance or feedback when necessary. Give students a few minutes to practice their presentations before finding another pair to present to. Make sure pairs are not presenting to each other about the same project. Tell all students to listen carefully and take notes while the other pairs present.

AFTER THE PROJECT

Have groups discuss each other's presentations. Ask them to decide which initiative they would most want to be part of. Have students comment on what was convincing or persuasive in the presentations they saw.

EXPLORE MORE

Have students watch Nadkarni's other TED Talk and complete a TED Talk summary worksheet (see page 9 of this Teacher's Guide). Ask them to offer their opinions about what she is doing, and whether they think it is helping the prisoners.

BRIGHT IDEAS

UNIT OVERVIEW

Reading: Students are introduced to simple, low-cost inventions helping people in the developing world.

TED Talk: Jane Chen introduces an invention that is saving the lives of premature babies in India.

Project: Students research a low-cost invention that is changing lives somewhere in the world.

Lesson 3A BIG PROBLEMS, SIMPLE SOLUTIONS

LESSON OVERVIEW

Aims:
- Read and comprehend an article about affordable inventions that are improving lives in poor countries.
- Understand key details and visuals.
- Make inferences.

Target Vocabulary: adjust, affordable, available, device, estimate, plentiful, portable, temporary

Reading Passage Summary: Students read an article featuring three low-cost and simple inventions that are saving lives around the world—from eyeglasses with lenses that can be adjusted by adding liquid, to a cheap device that makes a safer cooking fuel for burning indoors, to light and compact shelters that are easy to transport and set up during natural disasters. In each case, an affordable, low-tech item allows people the opportunity to live better lives.

TEACHING NOTES

THINK AND DISCUSS

For the first discussion question, brainstorm a list of famous inventions and write them on the board. Ask students what problems these inventions solved. Then put students in pairs or small groups to discuss the second question, and make a list of five modern-day problems that we don't have solutions for yet. Elicit from each group the problem that they ranked as number one, and write some on the board.

PRE-READING

Give students a few minutes to look at the infographic, pictures, and captions on pages 38–41 and answer the questions individually before comparing with a partner. Make sure students understand that they are guessing the answers and they do not need to be correct. After students read the article, have them come back and discuss their guesses. *Extension:* Ask pairs to discuss which invention might be the most important and explain why.

Think and Discuss

1. Answers will vary. Possibilities include: electricity, the Internet, the wheel, the printing press, the plow, etc. **2.** Answers will vary. Possibilities include: poverty, pollution, deforestation, illnesses, etc.

Pre-reading

A. Guesses will vary. Actual answers are: **Liquid Lenses 1.** They allow individuals to adjust the strength of the lenses of their own glasses.; **2.** You turn a dial on the side of the glasses and add or subtract liquid.

Understanding Key Details

Problem	Solution	Inventor	Main Material	Main Benefit
12. Not enough optometrists	1. Liquid lenses	*Joshua Silver*	6. Liquid	9. Easy to adjust lenses
4. Smoke from indoor cooking	10. Fuel briquettes	5. Amy Smith	2. Farm waste	*Cleaner burning*
11. Poor shelters for disaster victims	*Disaster shelters*	7. Michael McDaniel	8. Plastic	3. Lightweight and easy to transport

Understanding Visuals

1. a, c; **2. a.** 80; **b.** 8; **c.** 6; **3.** 2 minutes or less

Making Inferences

The following should be checked: 1, 3, 5, 6, 8

Building Vocabulary

A. 1. affordable; **2.** plentiful; **3.** adjust; **4.** estimates

Fuel Briquettes 1. to provide a safer form of fuel for indoor kitchen fires; **2.** in the developing world; **3.** farming families and those in their community **Disaster Shelters 1.** to provide homes that are easy to transport and assemble; **2.** in places where a natural disaster has destroyed people's homes; **3.** They provide an affordable way to begin to rebuild homes and communities after a natural disaster.

Getting the Main Ideas

1. a; **2.** a, b, d

B. 1. b; **2.** b; **3.** b; **4.** a

Getting Meaning from Context

A. a; **B.** They help people make money.

Critical Thinking

Answers will vary.

DEVELOPING READING SKILLS

GETTING THE MAIN IDEAS

A Have students read the entire passage either silently or while listening to the narrated passage on the audio. Have them work individually to answer the questions for Exercises A and B. Check answers as a class.

B. Ask students to find supporting evidence in the passage for each statement they choose. Elicit the evidence when checking answers as a class.

UNDERSTANDING KEY DETAILS

Point out that completing the information in the chart will give students a good chance to practice scanning for specific information. For a challenge, give them one minute to complete the entire chart. Have them check answers in pairs.

UNDERSTANDING VISUALS

Give students a few minutes to look over the diagram and read the information about the Exo shelter. Make sure students understand to put a check mark next to two answers for question 1. Note that for question 1, students should skim the diagram content, while questions 2 and 3 are good opportunities to practice scanning for specific information.

MAKING INFERENCES

Review the meaning of *inference*. Make sure students understand that an inference is implied from stated information, but not directly stated. Point out that even facts can be inferred, as is the case for option 1. The writer doesn't explain what an optometrist is, but students can easily infer from the previous sentence that an *eye doctor* and *optometrist* are the same thing. Note that option 2, while not stated in the passage, also cannot be inferred. The writer says that there are not enough optometrists, not that people can't afford them. Give students a few minutes to work individually to complete the activity. They will need enough time to go back to the passage to check the information about each point.

BUILDING VOCABULARY

A. Have students complete Exercise A individually before checking answers as a class. Explain that the verb *estimate* is mostly used when amounts or values are involved, such as estimating the cost of something, the distance to somewhere, or the amount of time that something will take.

B. Have students complete Exercise B individually before checking answers as a class. Some synonyms for *device* include *gadget, piece of equipment, tool, appliance.*

GETTING MEANING FROM CONTEXT

A. Give students a short time to look back at the use of the term in the passage (paragraph 2) and think about its meaning before writing their answers. Check answers as a class. Explain when you get an amount "down to" something else, it is being reduced. It is used when the drop in amount is intentional. In addition to price, the term is often used to talk about losing weight.

B. Have students discuss their ideas in pairs before checking answers as a class. An "economic benefit" will have a positive financial effect. The adjective *economic* tends to be used when the effects are more wide scale than affecting simply one person's finances.

CRITICAL THINKING

If possible, have students discuss in pairs or small groups of people from the same country. Then have them share their thoughts with the class. Ask students to give reasons why inventions would benefit people in their country specifically. If students are all from the same country, consider dividing them into groups by regions and choosing inventions useful for their regions or areas. **Extension:** To encourage more discussion, ask, *What are some other inventions that would benefit your country? Why?*

EXPLORE MORE

Have students work in pairs. Assign each pair one of the TED Talks to listen to, and have them complete a TED Talk summary worksheet (see page 9 of this Teacher's Guide). Then have them report back to a small group about what they learned from the talk. Each pair in the group should have listened to a different talk. Later in the unit, students can come back and study these TED Talks to learn about making successful presentations for their Project as well.

Lesson 3B — A WARM EMBRACE THAT SAVES LIVES

LESSON OVERVIEW

Aims:

- Watch and understand a talk about a simple invention that has the potential to affect millions of lives.
- Identify solutions and understand details.
- Visualize a process.

TED Talk summary: In her TED Talk, social entrepreneur Jane Chen introduces an invention that aims to save the lives of premature infants in India. The wrap that Chen's team created gives parents a low-tech, low-cost way to keep babies warm, replacing expensive incubators. Chen shows how teams like hers can make a difference in the world by identifying major problems and then working to find doable and low-cost solutions. An annotated transcript for the edited TED Talk is on pages 64–65 of this Teacher's Guide.

TEACHING NOTES

The short passage and questions introduce the problem that TED Talk speaker Jane Chen sets out to solve: the death and/or suffering of millions of premature infants in India. Because the premature babies cannot regulate their body temperature, and their parents are too far from hospitals with expensive incubators, they die or are afflicted with long-term health problems. Make sure students look over the definitions in the footnotes carefully, as the words will help them understand Chen's TED Talk.

1. She studied infant mortality in connection to premature babies.; **2.** If premature infants aren't warm enough, they don't develop normally, causing long-term health problems.; **3.** Expensive, high-tech solutions to health issues are not practical for people who live in rural areas, far away from hospitals.

PART 1

Previewing

A. electricity, rural, hot-water bottles, lightbulbs, unsafe

Identifying Solutions

A. Hot-water bottles and lightbulbs have been used in the past. These solutions perhaps work temporarily but don't succeed at regulating body heat over a long period of time, which is what is needed. Neither solution is the safest choice for a premature infant.

B. 2, 3, 6

Critical Thinking

1. The problems Chen describes also relate to the developing world and the affordability of certain technology.; **2.** Answers will vary.

PART 2

Understanding Details

1. b; **2.** a; **3.** It can be melted with only hot water and maintains the same temperature for four to six hours. It is an easy way to regulate the body temperature of the babies in need.

Visualizing a Process

1. phase-change material; **2.** 37 degrees, pocket; **3.** baby; **4.** 4–6 hours

Critical Thinking

When parents anticipate that their children will all survive as babies, they have fewer children.

PART 1

PREVIEWING

Have students work individually to complete the paragraph. Note that the paragraph further prepares students to understand the problem that Chen's invention solves.

IDENTIFYING SOLUTIONS

A. Play the video. Have students check their answers to Exercise A. Then have students discuss the questions in pairs. Note that while the solutions of using water bottles and light bulbs may help to keep the babies warm to some extent, both are ineffective in doing the job long term and can even be dangerous.

B. Have students work individually to complete the activity before comparing answers in pairs.
Extension: Ask pairs to use their own words to explain each important point again.

CRITICAL THINKING

1. Synthesizing. Have students discuss in pairs before eliciting a class discussion on the topics. Ask students to make a mind map or Venn diagram to compare the problems in Lessons A and B. Or elicit a class discussion and write a mind map or Venn diagram on the board.

2. Predicting. Students should be able to infer the general idea of Chen's invention by looking at the pictures on pages 45 and 48 and the diagram on page 48. Ask partners to share their predictions with the class.

PART 2

UNDERSTANDING DETAILS

Gives students one to two minutes to read the paragraph and answer the questions. Have students check answers in pairs. Point out that the questions all focus on identifying and understanding what phase-changing material is. Ask students to comment on why understanding this is important. *Extension:* Ask students to list all the important characteristics of the invention that Chen mentions. Then have them compare it to each point that Chen said was needed of the invention in Part 1 of her talk.

VISUALIZING A PROCESS

Have students work individually to complete the activity before checking answers in pairs.
Extension: Have partners practice explaining the process to each other in their own words. Encourage them to add sequence words such as *First, Then, Next* when explaining the process to each other.

CRITICAL THINKING

Interpreting Give students time to think about their answer to the question. Chen says it seems *counterintuitive* when explaining why her invention will help reduce population growth. Ask students to infer what she means by *counterintuitive*. Make sure they understand it means against what seems logical. She uses the term because usually we'd assume that by saving so many lives, populations would increase. However, Chen explains that when fewer babies are expected to die, it will slow population growth in India instead of increasing it because parents will have fewer children overall. (When parents expect that some of their children will die in infancy, they have more children.)

EXPLORE MORE

On the TED site, students can find an article from 2013 that is an update to Chen's 2010 TED Talk. She shares what her team learned from users of the Embrace wrap, and how they changed the product after listening to the opinions of mothers in India. She also talks about some unexpected cultural challenges they've faced in getting people to use the wraps.

Project   RESEARCHING LOW-COST INNOVATIONS

PROJECT OVERVIEW:

Aims:
- Students research a low-cost invention that solves a problem.
- Students explain the invention to their classmates in a two-minute presentation.
- Students listen and decide which invention is the most innovative.

Summary: Students watch a new TED Talk and use it to learn about another low-cost invention that is helping people to live better lives. They make a presentation about the invention to other pairs, and listen to other pairs present, too.

Materials: computer, Internet access, presentation software

Language Support: Showing interest: *Really?; That's interesting!; Wow!; That's amazing!*

TEACHING NOTES

PREPARATION

Have students work in pairs. Ask them to choose one of the TED Talks listed on page 49. Give them time to go to the TED site and decide which talk they're interested in watching. Or assign talks so that the topics are evenly distributed among the pairs. Explain that they should watch the talk, complete a TED Talk summary worksheet (see page 9 of this Teacher's Guide), and then organize a presentation with pictures, video, and information to introduce the invention to other pairs. Encourage them to search online for more information about the invention in addition to the TED Talk. Note the "Language Support" phrases on the board and review them before students begin the activity.

DURING THE PROJECT

After pairs choose their TED Talk, have them read through the questions before watching it. Tell them to take notes individually as they go, then discuss and combine their notes after they've finished watching. Or have partners choose different questions to answer while watching. Monitor as pairs prepare their presentations, and give assistance or feedback when necessary. Give students a few minutes to practice their presentations before finding two other pairs. Make sure pairs are not presenting about the same invention. Tell all students to listen carefully and take notes while the other pairs present.

AFTER THE PROJECT

Have pairs discuss what they learned in listening to each other's presentations. Encourage them to debate which invention is more innovative and useful, giving reasons and examples to support their opinions. *Extension:* Divide the class into teams based on which TED Talk pairs watched. Then have a class debate about which invention is the most innovative and why. Have each team present their ideas and opinions.

GAME CHANGERS

UNIT OVERVIEW

Reading: Students are introduced to research showing the benefits of playing games online.

TED Talk: Game designer Jane McGonigal talks about how playing games may be a way to solve global problems.

Project: Students create a proposal for a game with a social purpose.

Lesson 4A — IS GAMING GOOD FOR YOU?

LESSON OVERVIEW

Aims:
- Read and comprehend an article about how online gaming helps individuals develop important skills.
- Analyze pros and cons.
- Understand data.

Target Vocabulary: accomplishment, characteristics, cooperation, form, involved, predict, resource, significant

Reading Passage Summary: Students read about research that shows that gaming improves both social skills and thinking skills. In addition, students are introduced to the ideas of game designer Jane McGonigal, who believes that the optimism, team-building skills, and motivated productivity of gamers can be used to tackle the world's problems. She believes gamers may be the answer to solving some of the biggest global issues of the present day.

TEACHING NOTES

THINK AND DISCUSS

Have students discuss their answers in pairs before eliciting a class discussion about online gaming. Ask students who are gamers to share more about why they play. Ask others to share their thoughts about gaming and/or go over some typical preconceptions and criticism about gaming. Elicit a brainstorm of possible benefits of gaming. If necessary, draw a mind map on the board to organize discussion points.

PRE-READING

A. Have students look at the photo and read the caption on pages 52–53. Students may notice that the game is an online multiplayer game, which means that more than one person is playing at once. If students are unfamiliar with *World of Warcraft*, explain that it is a role-playing, adventure game. Elicit some possible benefits after students are finished discussing in pairs.

B. Note that students will answer more detailed questions based on the infographic later on in the lesson. Ask them to skim the information on page 54 to get the main idea of the infographic. After they answer question 1, have them focus on what's surprising to them.

C. Have students discuss in pairs before sharing their answers. Note that some students may have negative opinions about gaming. Encourage students to support their opinions with reasons and examples.

D. Remind students that to *skim* means to read quickly for the main idea. Skimming usually involves reading the first and last sentence of each paragraph, as well as looking at the title, picture, and headings in a passage to get the general idea of the content. However, in this case, Jane McGonigal's thoughts on gaming and gamers are only shared in the last two paragraphs of the passage.

DEVELOPING READING SKILLS

GETTING THE MAIN IDEAS

Have students read the entire passage, either silently or while listening to the narrated passage on the audio. Have them answer the questions for the activity. Check answers as a class. For question 2, ask students to share how they think gaming improves memory and planning. For question 3, elicit or explain the meaning of *virtuoso*. Students should understand that it refers to someone with extraordinary talents and skills, usually in music or art.

UNDERSTANDING KEY DETAILS

Have students work individually to go back through the reading to mark the sentences true or false before checking answers in pairs. Ask them to correct any false information.

ANALYZING PROS AND CONS

A. Have students work individually to complete the chart. Write the pro and con list on the board when eliciting answers. Remind students of their warm-up and pre-reading discussions. Ask them if the pros and cons presented by the writer are similar to the ones that they came up with.

B. Have students discuss in pairs. Note that the cons are only introduced at the very end of the article in the

conclusion, and each has clearly already been countered in the content of the passage.

UNDERSTANDING DATA

Give students three to five minutes to work individually to read in detail the data in the infographic and answer the questions. Check answers as a class. Note that areas where there are many active gamers likely have the resources and access to the technology necessary for daily gaming.

BUILDING VOCABULARY

A. Have students complete Exercise A individually before checking answers as a class. Note that *predict* contains the prefix *pre-*, which means "before." Elicit other words that contain the same prefix, such as *prefix, predate, precede, precaution*, etc.

B. Have students complete Exercise B individually before checking answers as a class. When used with verbs, the prefix *co-* indicates that something is done together.

GETTING MEANING FROM CONTEXT

Have students work individually to answer the questions. Then explain that someone who is "larger than life" usually has a much bigger personality than others. An experience or situation that is "larger than life" also is seen as a bigger and better version of regular life.

CRITICAL THINKING

Note that for question 1, students will mostly use their common sense to make inferences about older players, as it is not talked about in the passage and only the statistics are given in the infographic. As computer technology has become a regular part of our daily lives, many people have grown up playing games or online games as children. In addition, as games become more complex and challenging, they are more attractive to adults.

EXPLORE MORE

Students will listen to Jane McGonigal speak more about her thoughts about gamers and gaming in the Lesson B TED Talk.

Think and Discuss

1. Answers will vary. Popular types of online game include action games, sports-related games, role-play games, action-adventure games, simulation games, and strategy games; **2.** Answers will vary. Online gaming provides a social community and allows players to interact in the comfort of their own homes. Most gamers enjoy the entertainment and the challenge of playing online games.

Pre-reading

A. 1. Answers will vary. Successful players are often quick to react, smart strategists, and good collaborators.

B. 1. 1.2 billion gamers worldwide; 700 million online gamers; Western Europe and North America have the largest groups of active gamers.; **2.** Answers will vary.

C. Answers will vary.

D. Yes. McGonigal thinks the skills that gamers exhibit while playing games can be useful for solving world problems.

Getting the Main Ideas

1. Players work together toward the same goal. They also feel socially acceptable and less alone.; **2.** memory and planning; **3.** virtuoso gamers (those who play more than one hour every day)

Understanding Key Details

1. T; **2.** T; **3.** T; **4.** T; **5.** F

Analyzing Pros and Cons

A. 1. social/thinking skills; **2.** thinking/social skills; **3.** problem solvers; **4.** time/money; **5.** money/time; **6.** obesity

B. The article focuses mostly on the positive side, only offering negative points at the very end, which have already been disputed in the main content.

Understanding Data

1. 18 percent; **2.** 22 hours; **3.** North America and Europe; **4.** China; **5.** $70 billion; **6.** Answers will vary.

Building Vocabulary

A. 1. characteristics; **2.** significant; **3.** involved; **4.** predict

B. 1. b, c; **2.** c; **3.** b, c; **4.** a, c

Getting Meaning from Context

extraordinary; a person or experience that is better and more exciting than most

Critical Thinking

1. Answers will vary. Games have become more advanced and complicated, which likely attracts an older audience. And as the first generation of gamers gets older, they continue to play games as adults.; **2.** Answers will vary.

Lesson 4B GAMING CAN MAKE A BETTER WORLD

LESSON OVERVIEW

Aims:

• Watch and understand a talk about how gamers may be able to change the world.
• Summarize information.
• Recognize tone and message.

TED Talk Summary: In her TED Talk, Jane McGonigal shares her ideas about why gamers have the skills and drive to help the world become a better place. She says we should aspire to play more games to help people develop gamer "super powers," which can then be used to tackle real-world problems. An annotated transcript for the edited TED talk is on pages 66–67 of this Teacher's Guide.

TEACHING NOTES

Note that the information and questions serve as a follow up to what students have already learned about McGonigal and her ideas in Lesson A. Have students read the information and answer the questions in pairs.

1. She thinks that collectively we should spend 22 billion hours a week for ten years; **2.** global problems like poverty, climate change, and obesity

PART 1

Previewing

Gamers struggle to bring the same motivation that they have in online games to their work in the real world.

Getting the Main Ideas

A. Gamers don't believe they are as good at solving real-life problems as they are with problems in games. We give up quickly after failing, but in the game world we keep trying.

B. The following should be checked: overwhelmed, anxious, depressed, frustrated, cynical

C. Answers will vary. Possibilities include: the way they approach real-world problems; their motivation in the real world; their attitude about failure in real life.

Critical Thinking

She wants online games to influence how we behave and act in the world. She wants games to shape a new world by getting gamers to solve current major problems.

PART 2

Summarizing

World Without Oil

Problem: the world has run out of oil/has a shortage of oil; **Goal:** to survive an oil shortage; **Effect on Players:** many players keep habits they learned playing the game

Superstruct

Problem: humans have only 23 years left on the planet; **Goal:** to invent the future of energy, food, health, security, and the social safety net; **Effect on Players:** players came up with about 500 (insanely) creative solutions

Recognizing Tone and Message

1

Critical Thinking

1. Answers will vary; **2.** Answers will vary.

PART 1

PREVIEWING

Remind students of the four super powers outlined by McGonigal in Lesson A. These are skills exhibited by gamers in their virtual worlds, but not necessarily in their real lives. Elicit ideas as to why gamers may not be as successful using these skills in real life.

GETTING THE MAIN IDEAS

A. Have students read the question before playing the TED Talk. Point out that McGonigal will explain the meaning of "epic win" in her talk. Make sure students understand that McGonigal feels that in the game world, we're able to get back up after a failure, learn, get focused, and try again until we succeed and have an "epic win," but in real life we tend to stop after experiencing failure.

B. Have students check their answers in pairs. McGonigal says that with failure in real life come negative emotions. In the game world, these don't happen.

C. Have students work individually to complete the statement. Then elicit ideas about how McGonigal might be able to change the mindset of gamers.

CRITICAL THINKING

McGonigal means that her games are not trying to prepare people for world disasters; they are instead trying to equip gamers with the skills and motivation to make a difference in solving problems that are happening now.

PART 2

SUMMARIZING

Play the second part of the TED Talk. Tell students to focus on the information McGonigal gives about the two games. Have students check answers in pairs.

RECOGNIZING TONE AND MESSAGE

Have students read the paragraph and answer the questions individually. Make sure students understand that McGonigal is trying to change the way many people think about gamers—and also how gamers look at themselves and the role they can have in the real world.

CRITICAL THINKING

1. Reflecting. Give students time to review the concept map about each game before discussing their answers in pairs. Encourage them to give reasons and examples for their opinions.

2. Evaluating. Have students work individually to synthesize what they've learned in Lessons A and B. Ask them to form their final opinion before discussing with a partner.

EXPLORE MORE

McGonigal talks in more detail about how gamers are collaborative problem-solvers, and how they are motivated to get to work on a problem right away.

Project

CREATING A PROPOSAL FOR A NEW GAME

PROJECT OVERVIEW:

Aims
- Students create an online game that will help make a positive impact on a global issue.
- Students synthesize what they learned in the unit about gamers and their strengths.
- Students present their game proposals, listen to others, and choose one to support.

Summary: Students write a proposal for an online game that will help gamers change the world. Students present to two other pairs, who represent McGonigal's organization, The Institute for the Future. Groups then decide which game will have the most positive impact.

Materials: poster board, pens, tape, scissors, or computer and presentation software

Language Support: Talking about problems: *There are too many . . . ; There isn't/aren't enough . . .*

TEACHING NOTES

PREPARATION

Have students work in pairs to outline the specifics of the game. In deciding the global issue that their game focuses on, if necessary, have the class brainstorm a list of issues in addition to what's in the student book.

Make sure students are ready to explain the issue in their proposals. Note the "Language Support" phrases on the board and review them before students begin the activity.

DURING THE PROJECT

Have pairs work together to create their proposals. Point out that they should try to use persuasive language to win the votes of their audience. If students make posters, give them time to draw pictures and add information about the game and its purpose. Monitor as students work together to create their proposal. Then have pairs work with two other pairs to present their proposals. Make sure students explain the background to the problem their game focuses on, and how their game will help find a solution.

AFTER THE PROJECT

Have each group discuss the proposals presented, and debate which idea they want to develop into a real game. Tell them to think about the impact the game will have. After groups discuss, have them vote on the game they want to support. Then have group members give suggestions on how to make the game even better.

EXPLORE MORE

Have students work in pairs to find out about a real game with a social purpose.

LESSONS IN LEARNING

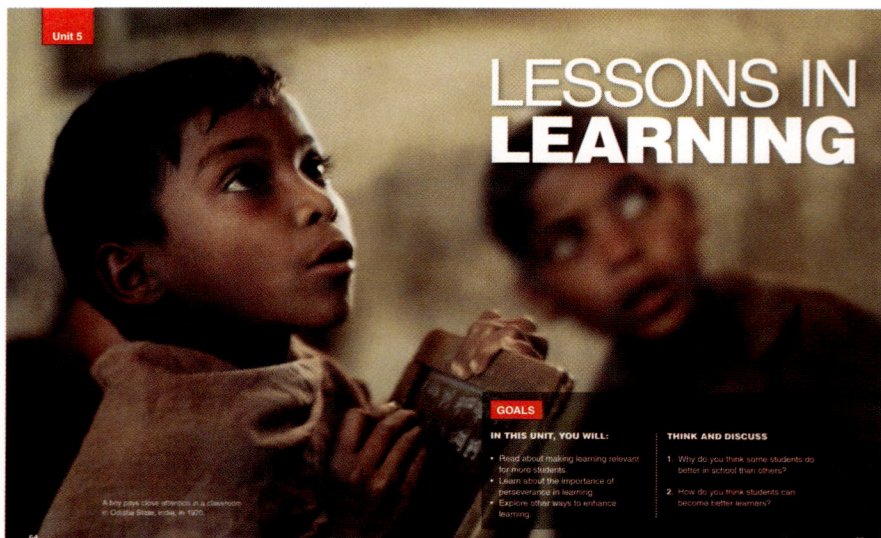

UNIT OVERVIEW

Reading: Students are introduced to the Studio School system, which combines traditional education with work experience.

TED Talk: Psychologist Angela Lee Duckworth talks about how her research shows that the deciding factor in success in school is not intelligence, but rather grit.

Project: Students conduct a survey and discuss factors related to success.

Lesson 5A ENGAGING LEARNERS

LESSON OVERVIEW

Aims:
- Read and comprehend an article about why some students don't feel engaged with school and how one school system is trying to change that.
- Support ideas with evidence.
- Find similarities and differences.

Target Vocabulary: approach, coach, combine, coach, determined, engaged, indicate, promising, relevant

Reading Passage Summary: Students read an article about why less than half of teenagers feel engaged with school. Many feel that what they are learning is not relevant for their lives and future work. In response to this, TED speaker Geoff Mulgan has created a new kind of school, the Studio School. These public schools in the United Kingdom all focus on combining general education with vocational training. Since the first Studio School was established, 40 more have opened.

TEACHING NOTES

THINK AND DISCUSS

Ask students to look at the picture and think about their own experiences with school and learning. Have students discuss their answers in pairs before leading a discussion with the class. This unit focuses on the idea that traditional education doesn't work for all students, and it explores efforts being made to change this. Encourage students to share what schools are like in their home countries, as well as their own personal learning styles.

PRE-READING

A. Give students one to two minutes to look over the charts on page 67 and write their answers individually. Have them share their answers with a partner. Then elicit some ideas, as a way of extending the Think and Discuss class discussion. Point out that the information in the poll is from the United States. Ask students to comment on whether they think it's the same for their home countries.

Think and Discuss

1. Answers will vary; **2.** Answers will vary.

Pre-reading

A. Answers will vary. As students get closer to the age of independence, when they'll find jobs and support themselves, many start to feel less connected to the school environment and the traditional learning process found in most schools.

B. 1. The Da Vinci School combines traditional education with practical on-the-job training.; **2.** It is likely that they don't have homework because they also have jobs.; **3.** A personal coach helps guide and advise an individual to help that person succeed, in this case at meeting their learning goals.

Getting the Main Ideas

1. teacher-centered, test-focused, academic learning; **2.** b; **3.** b; **4.** academic learning, practical training

Supporting Ideas with Evidence

1. 56 percent; **2.** one-third; **3.** 300; **4.** 80 percent; **5.** more than 40

Finding Similarities and Differences

Traditional Schools: c, d, e, j

Both: a, h

Studio Schools: b, f, g, i

Getting Meaning from Context

He means that what is normal is turned upside-down and changed completely.

Critical Thinking

1. Answers will vary; **2.** Answers will vary.

Building Vocabulary

A. relevant; approach; indicated; engage; determined

B. 1. b; **2.** c; **3.** a

Explore More

In Renaissance times, a studio was a place where learning and working were combined.

B. Give students a few minutes to read the information on page 68 and answer the questions. Note that *coach* is now commonly used as a job term in many areas outside of sport. It refers to a professional who instructs or trains people, usually one-on-one, with the aim of improving the success of that person in a certain area. In the last decade, jobs such as "life coach," "health coach," and "business coach" have become common. Check answers as a class.

C. Give students one minute to think about their answers before discussing in pairs. Note that students' ideas may vary widely depending on home countries and personal experiences. *Extension:* Have students work in pairs to write an outline of their ideal school. Tell them to focus especially on teaching and learning styles in that school. What is a typical classroom like? How do students and teachers interact? What options are there for learning outside of school? How often is homework assigned and tests given?

DEVELOPING READING SKILLS

GETTING THE MAIN IDEAS

Have students read the entire passage, either silently or while listening to the narrated passage on the audio.

Have them answer the questions individually before checking answers as a class. For question 1, elicit what the writer means. Ask students to explain in their own words.

SUPPORTING IDEAS WITH EVIDENCE

Elicit a review of the types of evidence students might encounter in a paragraph: quotes, statistics, stories, etc. Ask students what kinds of evidence the questions in the activity focus on (statistics). Point out that this is a good opportunity to practice scanning for answers. Have students work individually to complete the activity before checking answers in pairs.

FINDING SIMILARITIES AND DIFFERENCES

Review how to make and use a Venn diagram. Point out that it's especially useful for comparison and contrast, or listing similarities and differences. Give students a few minutes to complete the diagram individually before comparing answers in pairs. Ask students to raise their hands to show which kind of school they'd rather attend. Note that they will discuss this question in more detail in Critical Thinking. *Extension:* Have students work individually to write a paragraph that compares and contrasts the two types of schools using the information in the Venn diagram.

GETTING MEANING FROM CONTEXT

Explain that getting meaning from context can involve understanding an unknown word by getting clues from the author or by making a guess based on common sense. The author uses the phrase at the end of the passage, after readers already understand about the Studio School and how different it is from a traditional school. Students should be able to guess that to "turn (something) on its head" refers to changing something completely.

CRITICAL THINKING

1. Personalizing. Have students discuss their opinions in pairs. Ask them to offer reasons and examples to support their thoughts and ideas. Then open up the discussion to the class, eliciting both pros and cons about the Studio School. Note that students will have different learning styles, and their responses to this question will depend somewhat on how they learn best. **Extension:** Have students describe to each other their ideal teacher. How does this teacher help them learn better?

2. Reflecting. Have students share their ideas in pairs. Tell them to think about their own experiences as teenagers and how they felt about school and how they felt about learning. Then have students share their opinions with the class.

BUILDING VOCABULARY

A. Have students complete Exercise A individually before checking answers as a class. The verb *engage* also appears in the lesson in noun form, *engagement* (in the diagram on page 67), and adjective form, *engaged* (page 67). It is also part of the passage title: *Engaging* Learners. **Extension:** Have students write new sentences for each form of the word *engage*.

B. Have students complete Exercise B individually before checking answers as a class.

EXPLORE MORE

To learn more about Geoff Mulgan and Studio Schools, have students watch Mulgan's TED Talk while completing a TED Talk summary worksheet (see page 9 of this Teacher's Guide).

| Lesson 5B | **THE KEY TO SUCCESS? GRIT** |

LESSON OVERVIEW

Aims:
- Watch and understand a talk about what might be the most common factor for success: grit.
- Understand terms.
- Summarize a talk.

TED Talk Summary: In her TED Talk, psychologist and academic Angela Lee Duckworth explains her research about what makes people successful, especially in schools. When she worked as a teacher, she realized that the smartest students are often not the most successful ones. And after setting out to research why, she came to the conclusion that one thing matters more than any other in success: grit. The students who do well are the ones who persevere, and keep in mind long-term goals. An annotated transcript for the edited TED talk is on pages 68–69 of this Teacher's Guide.

TEACHING NOTES

The opening passage and questions introduce both Duckworth and the background of her research about learning. Note that although the paragraphs do not state directly her ideas about grit, students should be able to infer from the lesson title what the "one factor" is. Have students read the paragraphs individually before writing their answers. Then have them check answers in pairs.

PART 1

Previewing

Have students complete the activity individually. If necessary, explain what *I.Q.* refers to. A student's *intelligence quotient* is calculated from a test, and most people have a score between 85 and 115. A person's I.Q. is supposed to measure their mental agility. In many countries, I.Q. scores, usually

1. The smartest kids are not the ones who get the best grades; 2. There is one factor that affects engagement in school; 3. People are excited by her ideas. Her various honors and grants demonstrate this.

PART 1

Previewing

Answers will vary somewhat. Duckworth says that the students who do well in school are often not the smartest ones. And some of her worst learners were in contrast very smart individuals.

Getting the Main Idea

The following should be checked: 1, 3, 6

Critical Thinking

Answers will vary. She reveals in the second part of her talk that grit is the major factor affecting success.

PART 2

Understanding the Overall Message

1. c; **2.** c

Understanding Terms

1. a, b; 2. When students realize that the human brain grows in response to challenges, they are more likely to keep trying when a challenge or difficulty arises.

Summarizing the Talk

e, c, a, f, b, d

Getting Meaning from Context

She means that we must see life as a long journey with ups and downs that we must persevere through instead of expecting quick and easy success.

Critical Thinking

1. Both say that traditional learning is not the best for all students. Duckworth focuses on a character trait that she wants to develop more in students, while Mulgan focuses on how schools can engage learners by changing the way teaching and learning happen; **2.** Answers will vary. However, Duckworth researched various areas of life and found grit was the key factor for success in all of them.

Explore More

In her research at Chicago public schools, she discovered that grittier kids were more likely to graduate.

---

accessed when students are young, are the traditional standard for shaping a student's path in a school system. For example, a student with a higher I.Q. might be put in more challenging classes.

GETTING THE MAIN IDEA

Have students read the excerpt before playing the video. Then give them one or two minutes to complete the activity before checking answers in pairs.

CRITICAL THINKING

Predicting. Give students a few minutes to discuss their ideas with a partner. Encourage students to use what they read and discussed in Lesson A to help them predict what Duckworth is going to say. Tell students to also talk about what they find useful for success in learning. Point out that students are experts here, since they are students.

PART 2

UNDERSTANDING THE OVERALL MESSAGE

Have students read the questions first. Then play the video. Have them circle the answers as they watch. Check answers as a class, eliciting a definition of *grit* in students' own words. Note that having grit is usually associated with having a certain strength of character, which that person uses to keep going in tough times.

UNDERSTANDING TERMS

Have students work individually to read the paragraph and answer the questions. If necessary, play the video again.

SUMMARIZING THE TALK

Have students work individually or in pairs to read through each point and choose the correct sequence. Then play the video again to have students check their answers.

GETTING MEANING FROM CONTEXT

Have students work individually to write their ideas before discussing their answers with a partner. Tell them to think about the experience of running a marathon. Ask students to first comment on how people who run marathons have grit before sharing their thoughts about how people who do well in life have grit, too.

CRITICAL THINKING

1. Synthesizing. Have students discuss in pairs, giving reasons for their answers. Then encourage a class discussion to have students share their thoughts and opinions. Encourage students to make a Venn diagram to note the similarities and differences between the two, or draw one on the board as students share points.

2. Reflecting. Have students work in groups of three or four. Ask them to share one other area of life where they think grit is useful and why. Encourage them to share personal stories to support their opinions if possible.

EXPLORE MORE

Duckworth did not only research schools to study the correlation between grit and success. Ask students what other places she talks about where grit was the deciding factor in success.

Project — PREPARING A SURVEY ON SUCCESS

PROJECT OVERVIEW:

Aims:
- Students conduct a survey about factors necessary for success in life.
- Students report their findings to the class, and reflect together on the findings.

Summary: Students interview people to hear their ideas about factors for success. Then pairs then report their findings to the class.

Materials: paper/notebook, pen

Language Support: Asking about opinions: *What do you think about . . . ? How do you feel about . . . ? What are your thoughts on . . . ?*

TEACHING NOTES

PREPARATION

Have students work in pairs to share their ideas about what factors contribute to success. Have students use this time to form their ideas and practice expressing them. Tell them to also prepare how to ask others their thoughts on success. Note the "Language Support" phrases above on the board, and review them before students begin the activity.

DURING THE PROJECT

Students can conduct their survey either with classmates or with friends or family outside class time. If the activity is carried out in class, give students five to ten minutes to do this part of the project. They must meet with at least two other pairs and note the responses they obtain. Then have pairs sit down again to organize the information they heard and collected from their fellow students. Tell them to outline their findings. Then have each pair report to the class.

AFTER THE PROJECT

Have a class discussion about the findings. Note common factors and differing ones. Ask students to share their reasons for believing certain factors are important. Elicit any personal stories that students are willing to share. Ask students if the information in the unit changed their minds about learning and success at all. If so, how?

EXPLORE MORE

Have students go to TED.com to watch Rita Pierson's engaging talk and complete a TED Talk summary worksheet (see page 9 of this Teacher's Guide). She says that students need support from and connection with their teachers in order to do well in school and life.

FOOD FOR LIFE

Elementary school children choose healthy foods at a school cafeteria in Hagerstown, Maryland, U.S.A.

FOOD FOR LIFE

GOALS

IN THIS UNIT, YOU WILL:
- Read about how a celebrity chef wants people to eat better.
- Learn about problems with the food served in some schools.
- Explore ways to encourage healthy eating.

THINK AND DISCUSS
1. What kinds of foods do you like to eat? Do you think your diet is healthy?
2. What problems can people have if they eat the wrong foods?

UNIT OVERVIEW

Reading: Students are introduced to the crisis of poor diet in the United States and chef Jamie Oliver's attempts to fix it.

TED Talk: Oliver focuses on how the processed food served in school lunches is creating a health disaster for future generations across the United States and what he is doing to stop it.

Project: Students create an event for Oliver's food revolution and advertise it with a flyer.

Lesson 6A   FOOD REVOLUTION

LESSON OVERVIEW

Aims:
- Read and comprehend an article about chef Jamie Oliver's mission to change eating habits in the United States.
- Identify problems and solutions.
- Understand infographics.

Target Vocabulary: awareness, consumers, nutrition, participate, replace, revolution, urge, widespread

Reading Passage Summary: Students read about British chef Jamie Oliver's efforts to change the eating habits of people in Huntington, West Virginia, the unhealthiest city in the United States. Oliver believes that the problem of obesity and poor nutrition in the United States is a result of people becoming disconnected from real food. Processed and fast food have become the norm, and this has led to an epidemic of obesity and food-related illnesses. Oliver hopes to change the way people eat by educating them about food, teaching them how to cook, and getting supermarkets and food businesses to act more responsibly.

TEACHING NOTES

THINK AND DISCUSS

Have students work individually to write a list of foods they eat daily. Then have them compare in pairs and talk about their favorite foods first, before discussing whether they eat a healthy diet or not. Then lead a class discussion for question 2 to brainstorm some problems related to bad nutrition.

PRE-READING

A. Note that students will analyze the infographic in more detail later in the lesson. For Exercise A, encourage them to scan for the answers. To be *out of touch* with someone or something means to have lost contact and connection.

B. Have students work individually before discussing their answers in pairs. Students should be able to infer that Huntington's health issues have something to do with food and people's eating habits there. For question 2, elicit students' ideas about what a *food revolution* might be.

Think and Discuss

1. Answers will vary.; **2.** Answers will vary. Possibilities include: headaches, joint problems, digestive problems, illnesses like cancer and diabetes, limited ability to concentrate, mood swings, etc.

Pre-reading

A. 1. United States, England, Australia; **2.** Kids don't understand about individual foods because the meals they eat are processed.

B. 1–2. Predictions will vary. Actual answers are:
1. In 2009, Huntington had the highest obesity rate in America.; **2.** Oliver's movement aims to improve people's eating habits and health.

Understanding the Main Ideas

A. 1

B. He wants people to use fresh ingredients and stay away from processed foods.

Identifying Problems and Solutions

A. Problems: 2, 3, 4; **Solutions:** 5, 6

B. Problems with Food and Eating

At Home: not learning about food, cooking, and eating; dinners not cooked with fresh ingredients anymore; convenience foods have replaced homemade meals

At School: not learning about food, cooking, and eating; processed foods common; unhealthy food mass-produced; low cost of food valued over nutrition

On Main Street: not learning about food, cooking, and eating; fast food is too high in sugar and fat; portion sizes in restaurants are too big; food labeling is unclear in supermarkets

C. home cooks share simple recipes with each other; supermarkets become "food ambassadors"; food brands provide better labeling; schools serve healthier meals

Understanding Infographics

1. fruits and vegetables; **2.** out of (the) home; **3.** won't know how to cook; **4.** year; **5.** sick

Building Vocabulary

A. 1. replace; **2.** nutrition; **3.** urge; **4.** consumer

B. 1. c; **2.** a; **3.** –; **4.** d; **5.** b; **6.** –

Getting Meaning from Context

1. to start to do something regularly in your daily life
2. Answers will vary, but convenience foods are not prepared from fresh ingredients and are usually processed. Possibilities include: any fast food, junk food like potato chips, frozen foods, foods made from processed ingredients like hot dogs, etc.

Critical Thinking

1. Answers will vary.; **2.** Answers will vary. Possibilities include: Encourage customers at the supermarket to use fresh ingredients by holding cooking classes, offering demonstrations, and sharing recipes; ensuring the supermarket sells products with clear labeling.

Explore More

The centers teach topics such as cooking skills, how to make easy homemade meals, food shopping skills, etc.

DEVELOPING READING SKILLS

UNDERSTANDING THE MAIN IDEAS

A. Have students read the entire passage, either silently or while listening to the narrated passage on the audio. Have them work individually to answer the questions for Exercise A before checking answers in pairs.

B. Have students write their answers individually before checking as a class. The passage explains various ways in which Oliver is attempting to change the way Americans interact with food, including eating, cooking, and shopping. He discusses the ways individuals, companies, and schools can help Americans eat more healthily.

IDENTIFYING PROBLEMS AND SOLUTIONS

A. Have students work individually or in pairs to complete Exercise A before checking answers as a class. Use this as an opportunity to look at the organization of ideas in the passage. The writer presents the problems first, and then Oliver's solutions.

B. Give students a few minutes to work individually to complete the concept map. Explain that instead of full sentences, students should write short notes in their own words on the map. Note that students' wording will differ, so encourage them to compare their general ideas in pairs when checking answers. Or check answers as a class, writing the concept map on the board while eliciting each point.

C. Note that students can also write their ideas for solutions on the concept map, making new branches for each topic in Exercise B. Have students work individually to find the solutions, then check answers as a class.

UNDERSTANDING INFOGRAPHICS

Give students a few minutes to read the infographic in detail and complete the activity. Check answers as a class. Elicit or explain the information, when necessary. For example, *food that doesn't come from a box* refers to eating homemade meals (instead of fast food). When a certain topic is *compulsory education* in a country, it means that it is required by law to be taught in schools. Food eaten *out of home* includes food bought at restaurants, convenience stores, and fast-food diners.

BUILDING VOCABULARY

A. Have students complete Exercise A individually before checking answers as a class. Note that while *nutrition* is generally used to talk about eating well and the benefits we get from food, it is also used to refer to the science that studies these same topics.

B. Have students complete Exercise B individually before checking answers as a class. Traditionally, the word *revolution* is used to describe the event of a government being overthrown. However, it is also used to describe a dramatic change in an aspect of everyday life.

GETTING MEANING FROM CONTEXT

A. *Getting into the habit* of something usually takes a little time. It is not an instant change of ways, but one that comes from repeating a new action again and again. You make it a new habit by doing it frequently.

B. Have students work individually or in pairs to brainstorm a list of convenience foods. Tell them to focus on foods that they eat. Then elicit examples from the class.

CRITICAL THINKING

Have students discuss the questions in pairs before eliciting a class discussion for each. Encourage students to give reasons and examples for their opinions.

1. Applying. Point out that both bad and good habits are mentioned in the passage, and students can talk about either or both in relation to their own habits.

2. Reflecting. Tell students to imagine a "food ambassador" at their local supermarket. What would that person's job involve?

EXPLORE MORE

Oliver's Ministry of Food has four centers in England. Each offers educational outreach to the local community, similar to his center in Huntington.

Lesson 6B TEACH EVERY CHILD ABOUT FOOD

LESSON OVERVIEW

Aims:
- Watch and understand a talk about how to address the problem of poor nutrition in schools in the United States.
- Identify main ideas and key details.

TED Talk Summary: In his TED Talk, TED prize-winner Jamie Oliver goes into detail about problems with the nutritional standards in schools across the United States. Oliver shows us how the current set-up for school nutrition is broken, and how to fix it. First, educating kids about food is imperative. Second,

schools must serve lunches made from fresh ingredients. Third, kids need to learn how to cook. And lastly, Oliver says that important decision-makers have to support this movement for there to really be long-term change. An annotated transcript for the edited TED Talk is on pages 70–71 of this Teacher's Guide.

TEACHING NOTES

Have students work individually to read the paragraphs and answer the questions. Encourage them to also use what they've already learned about Oliver in Lesson A. Check answers as a class, using questions 2 and 3 to encourage a discussion about Oliver's overall goals.

1. His parents owned a restaurant and pub.; **2.** funding; **3.** to educate people about food and improve their lives

PART 1

Previewing

A. 1. c; **2.** e; **3.** f; **4.** a; **5.** b; **6.** d

B. 1. purpose; **2.** health; **3.** kids; **4.** important

Getting the Main Idea

B. 1. if they don't know what it is, they won't eat it; **2.** educating kids about food in schools

PART 2

Previewing

Predictions will vary. He is showing the audience how much sugar schoolchildren consume from drinking flavored milk two times a day.

Getting the Main Idea

1. flavorings, colorings, and sugar; **2.** so kids will drink it; **3.** the same amount; **4.** He thinks giving flavored milk to children is a bad idea.

Critical Thinking

1. Children who get used to eating without cutlery will think eating fast food is normal.

2. Answers will vary.

PART 3

Understanding Key Details

A. The following should be checked or circled: 1, 4

B. Answers will vary. Oliver seems to feel very strongly about what he is saying

Critical Thinking

Answers will vary.

PART 1

PREVIEWING

A. Have students complete Exercise A individually before checking answers in pairs. Ask students to discuss which vegetables from the list they eat most often, and how they are prepared.

B. Have students work individually to complete Exercise B. Note that students will check answers in **Getting the Main Idea**. If necessary, elicit or explain the meaning of *arm us with the tools* and *haven't really evolved*.

GETTING THE MAIN IDEA

A. Play the video. Have students check their answers as they watch.

B. Give students a minute to work individually to write their answers before checking answers with a partner.

PART 2

PREVIEWING

Have students discuss their answers in pairs. Note that students' predictions may not be correct, but encourage them to consider the theme of the unit, as well as the title of Part 2 while making their guesses.

Have students check their answers while watching the video in **Getting the Main Idea**.

GETTING THE MAIN IDEA

Have students read the questions carefully and work individually or in pairs discuss answers before watching the video. Then play the video and have students check their answers.

CRITICAL THINKING

1. Inferring. Have students discuss in pairs, giving ideas and examples. Note that Oliver's comments about cutlery are in Part 1 of his talk. He points out that most fast food is made to be eaten with your hands, not utensils. If necessary, replay Part 1 before students answer question 1.

2. Evaluating. Check answers as a class. Showing the audience the wheelbarrow and pouring the sugar on the stage gives impact to his message about the amount of sugar children get from milk in school.

PART 3

UNDERSTANDING KEY DETAILS

A. Have students work individually to read the paragraphs and complete Exercise A. Point out that students should refer to the definitions in the footnotes to understand what Oliver is saying, if necessary. Have them check their answers as they watch the video in Exercise B.

B. After students discuss in pairs, have them share their answers with the class. Oliver is a very high-energy speaker. This is clearly a topic that he is passionate and therefore emotional about. At the end of the talk, he speaks about how meaningful the TED prize is to him. We can hear Oliver taking deep breaths to control his emotions.

CRITICAL THINKING

Give students time to work individually to write their lists. Point out that they don't need to already know how to make these meals. Tell them to focus on Oliver's message (cooking healthy, fresh, simple food) when composing their lists. Then have students share and compare their lists with a partner.

EXPLORE MORE

Encourage students to also find video clips online from Oliver's TV series *Food Revolution*, which took place in Huntington, West Virginia.

Project	# PLANNING AN EVENT TO PROMOTE FOOD REVOLUTION DAY

PROJECT OVERVIEW:

Aims
- Students organize an event for Oliver's Food Revolution and create a flyer to advertise it.
- Students analyze each other's advertisements and decide which event to join.

Summary: Students research about and organize an event for Oliver's Food Revolution Day. They make a flyer to advertise it. They hang their flyers around the classroom and walk around to view each other's advertisements and decide which event to join.

Materials: poster board or paper, marker or color pens, or computer and printer

Language Support: Making and replying to suggestions: *Let's . . . ; Sounds good; I don't know . . . ; That's a good idea.*

TEACHING NOTES

PREPARATION

Have students work in pairs. Ask them to review the event ideas in the student book and brainstorm some additional ideas. After pairs have chosen their event, have them go online to learn more about Food Revolution Day. Tell them to look for information about

similar events to get ideas. Point out that their advertisements should be persuasive. Note the "Language Support" phrases above on the board and review them before students begin the activity.

DURING THE PROJECT

Have pairs make a flyer to advertise their event. Ask them to think about how to make the event sound appealing. Give students five to ten minutes to complete their flyers. Then have students post their flyers around the classroom. Give students five to ten minutes to walk around and read each other's flyers. Tell students to think about which event they would like to attend and why.

AFTER THE PROJECT

Have students share their answers to the questions in the student book in pairs before discussing their opinions and ideas as a class. Ask students to support their opinions with reasons and examples.

EXPLORE MORE

Have students search online to learn more about recent Food Revolution Day events at foodrevolutionday.com. Note the website foodrevolution.org is run by a separate organization and is not connected to Oliver's.

BODY SIGNS

Medalists celebrate at the 2014 Winter Olympics in Sochi, Russia.

**BODY
SIGNS**

GOALS

IN THIS UNIT, YOU WILL:

- Read about the power of nonverbal communication.
- Learn how we can use our bodies to change our attitudes.
- Explore low- and high-power poses.

THINK AND DISCUSS

1. What are some examples of body language?
2. What kinds of messages do we send through our body language?

UNIT OVERVIEW

Reading: Students read about how our body language affects other people's perceptions of us and our perception of ourselves.

TED Talk: Social scientist Amy Cuddy shares what her research and experience have taught her about the power of "faking it till you make it."

Project: Students try an experiment similar to Cuddy's to see if striking different poses affects their performance in a presentation.

Lesson 7A INSPIRED LEADERSHIP

LESSON OVERVIEW

Aims:

- Read and comprehend an article about how high-power and low-power poses affect how you feel.
- Get main ideas and key details.
- Understand references.

Target Vocabulary: confident, conversely, cope, favorably, prove, qualifications, releases, stress

Reading Passage Summary: Students read about social scientist Amy Cuddy's research on how our body language affects how we view ourselves. She ran an experiment in which two groups of people are interviewed for a job. One group practiced high-power poses before the interview and the other did low-power poses. The high-power group performed markedly better in the interview. Cuddy explains that our brains actually react to our body language by releasing chemicals that affect how we feel.

TEACHING NOTES

THINK AND DISCUSS

Ask students to look closely at the picture on pages 92–93. Elicit descriptions of the body language of each team. Have students discuss the questions in pairs before continuing the class discussion.

PRE-READING

A. Give students a minute or so to think about and write their answers before discussing with a partner. Point out that Bolt's body language is the same as the winning team on the previous page.

B. Give students a few minutes to look over the infographic together. Focus them on the four different colored poses at the bottom of the infographic first. They should be able to match the green pose to that of Usain Bolt.

Think and Discuss

1. Answers will vary. Possibilities include: posture, gestures, eye contact, etc.; **2.** Answers will vary. Students will learn in the unit that we convey messages about our power through body language.

Pre-reading

A. 1. Answers will vary. Possibilities include: triumphant, victorious, happy, joyous, strong, powerful, proud, etc.

B. 1. Bolt is making a tall-and-proud pose that shows strength.; **2.** The infographic shows us how people see us and how we view ourselves while using various non verbal expressions.

C. c

D. a; In skimming, students should note that each paragraph begins with information and evidence about the research. Students should also pick up vocabulary that helps them infer that the topic is research.

Getting the Main Ideas

1. b; **2. a.** the way we view ourselves and are viewed by others; **b.** people performed well in an interview; **c.** people didn't perform well in an interview

Getting Key Details

A. 1. it may be; **2.** not told; **3.** no difference at all; **4.** brain

B. nonverbal communication

Recognizing the Structure of a Text

A. 1. method; **2.** conclusion; **3 .** hypothesis; **4.** results

B. High-Power Pose: powerful, confident, positively **Low-Power Pose:** powerless, stressed and less positive, negatively

Building Vocabulary

A. 1. stressed; **2.** cope; **3.** releases; **4.** confident

B. 1. b; **2.** a; **3.** d; **4.** c

Critical Thinking

1. She means the energy and manner with which they present themselves to others. **2.** Answers will vary.

C. Have students discuss their ideas in groups. Most should be able to infer from the work they did in **Think and Discuss** that a power pose refers to body language that makes us feel powerful.

D. Have students answer individually before checking answers as a class. Elicit how students recognized that it was an article about research. While skimming, students should have read the first sentence of each paragraph, and picked up words like *social scientist, experiment, biological explanation, research*.

DEVELOPING READING SKILLS

GETTING THE MAIN IDEAS

Have students read the entire passage, either silently or while listening to the narrated passage on the audio. Have them answer the questions for Exercise A individually before checking as a class. For question 2, students' answers may vary slightly. Encourage them to use their own words.

GETTING KEY DETAILS

A. Have students work individually to complete the activity before checking answers in pairs.

B. Have students work individually to complete the activity before checking answers together.

RECOGNIZING THE STRUCTURE OF A TEXT

A. Give students a minute or two to carefully read the paragraph. If necessary, elicit the meaning of each term: *hypothesis, method, results, conclusion*. Have students work individually to complete the activity before checking answers in pairs.

B. Make sure students understand that the diagram is explaining what happens when chemicals are released in the brain for each pose. Encourage students to write the answers in their own words. Have them work individually before checking answers in class.

BUILDING VOCABULARY

A. Have students do Activity A individually before checking answers as a class. Note that the adjective form of *stress* is *stressed*. There are numerous ways to express being in a state of stress: *I am stressed out; I am under a lot of stress; This is stressful; I'm feeling stressed.*

B. Have students complete Exercise B individually before checking answers as a class.

CRITICAL THINKING

Give students a minute to think about their answers in pairs before sharing with a partner. Then elicit students' ideas for a class discussion.

1. Analyzing. While *presence* literally means the state of existing, the term is used to describe a person's energy, manner, and appearance. If someone has a *good presence*, it usually means others immediately have a positive impression of them.

2. Personalizing. Encourage students to think about people they know as well as famous people like celebrities and politicians. Tell them to explain what stands out about that person's body language and what kind of impression it creates.

EXPLORE MORE

Tell students to do an online search using terms such as: *low-power poses, body language, nonverbal expressions, gestures,* etc.

Lesson 7B # YOUR BODY LANGUAGE SHAPES WHO YOU ARE

LESSON OVERVIEW

Aims:
• Watch and understand a talk about how our nonverbal expressions can change our lives.
• Get the main point.
• Recognize sequence.

TED Talk Summary: In her TED Talk, Amy Cuddy explains her research of nonverbal expressions. She looks not only at how others perceive us because of our body language, but also at how we see ourselves. Cuddy explains how changing our body language and practicing power poses can help us become a more confident and powerful person. An annotated transcript for the edited TED Talk is on pages 72–73 of this Teacher's Guide.

TEACHING NOTES

The paragraphs introduce the speaker and how she ended up studying body language. Have students read the information before answering the questions.

PART 1

PREVIEWING

A. Have students complete Exercise A individually before checking answers in pairs.

GETTING THE MAIN IDEAS

Have students read the questions and answer choices. Then play the video. Elicit students' ideas about question 1. Note that many of the nonverbal expressions from politicians that she shows are not positive.

CRITICAL THINKING

Give students a minute to think about their answers before discussing in pairs.

PART 2

GETTING THE MAIN POINT

A. Give students a minute to read the excerpt and think about the meaning of the phrase before comparing their answers with a partner. Point out that Cuddy actually explains the meaning in the sentence that follows "Can you fake it till you make it?" Ask students to put her explanation in their own words.

B. Play the video. Then have students work individually to answer the question. Ask students to raise their hands if they agree so far with what Cuddy is saying.

CRITICAL THINKING

Have students discuss in pairs before eliciting a class discussion. Cuddy is saying that people who feel more powerful have a higher risk tolerance. There are many areas in life where having a high risk tolerance is beneficial. Examples include starting a new business, or applying for a better position at work.

1. She was involved in a car accident.; **2.** Her male MBA students had different body language from her female students, and were more successful.;
3. Answers will vary. It is a topic that crosses many disciplines and areas of life. Cuddy offers some easy ideas about improving your power, which may appeal to many.

PART 1

Previewing

A. 2

Getting the Main Ideas

1. She is showing what body language can reveal about someone and how it can change our perception of that person.; **2.** a; **3.** how we judge others; how they judge us; **4.** She means ourselves. The way we think about ourselves is also influenced by our body language.

Critical Thinking

Answers will vary. Cuddy focuses especially on public presentations. Other possibilities include: meeting people for the first time, dates, or job interviews.

PART 2

Getting the Main Point

A. To "fake it till you make it" means to pretend to be good at something until you actually are.

B. b

Critical Thinking

People who feel powerful have a higher tolerance for risk. Confident people are more comfortable with risk.

PART 3

Recognizing Sequence

a. 4; **b.** 7; **c.** 2; **d.** 6; **e.** 1; **f.** 5; **g.** 3

Understanding Key Details

A. These people probably feel uncormfortable pretending to be something they are not. Cuddy's point though is that in pretending to be that something, you actually become it.

B. 1. b; **2.** to fake it; **3.** She became more confident and the kind of student she wanted to be.

Identifying Purpose

b, c

Summarizing

power-posing, powerless, high-power, outcome

Critical Thinking

1. In this case, the student did not just experience success at what she wanted to do, she changed her personality and became the type of high-power person that she wanted to be. As a result, she changed her life.

2. Answers will vary.

PART 3

RECOGNIZING SEQUENCE

A. Give students a minute to read the statements first. Then play the video and have students complete Exercise A.

UNDERSTANDING KEY DETAILS

A. Give students time to think about and write their answers individually before discussing with a partner. Explain that the first part of "fake it till you make it" requires a person to act and behave differently to their true feelings.

B. Play the video. Have students work individually to complete the activity as they watch before checking answers in pairs.

IDENTIFYING PURPOSE

Make sure students understand to choose two answers. Have students complete the activity individually before checking answers as a class. Elicit each example that Cuddy has given in her speech about faking till you make it: the experiment, her own story, and the story of her students.

SUMMARIZING

Have students work individually before checking answers as a class. Ask students to comment on why they think Cuddy says two minutes is enough time.

CRITICAL THINKING

Have students discuss in pairs before eliciting a class discussion.

1. Inferring. In this case, it is a slight change in wording that gives the statement a more dramatic meaning. Usually, the idea of "fake it till you make it" is referring to learning to do a specific skill or ability, but when Cuddy changes "make" to "become," she shifts the meaning to being about transforming yourself. By pretending to be a certain kind of person, one with power and confidence, you eventually become that.

2. Reasoning. Make sure students understand that to "believe in" someone means to support them and encourage them to succeed. Note that Cuddy would say that what we believe about ourselves has a more significant impact on our lives, and so believing in ourselves is key.

EXPLORE MORE

Have students watch Cuddy's full talk online while completing a TED Talk summary worksheet (see page 9 of this Teacher's Guide).

Project | # PRACTICING POWER POSES

PROJECT OVERVIEW

Aims:
- Students practice power poses before giving a presentation.
- Students try out and evaluate what they learned in the TED Talk.
- Students discuss their experiences.

Summary: Students give a brief presentation on power posing. Before presenting, they practice either low-power or high-power poses. The judges then try to guess which presenter did which pose based on their presentations. Students then discuss how they felt and what they learned in the process of trying out Cuddy's ideas.

Materials: examples of Cuddy's power poses, access to the Internet, presentation software

Language Support: Agreeing or Disagreeing: *I think . . . ; I agree because . . . ; I disagree. In my opinion . . .*

TEACHING NOTES

PREPARATION

Have students work in pairs. Tell them to look over the poses in the pictures on the page and in the infographic in Lesson A. Remind them to find both high-power and low-power poses. Explain that in their presentations they can summarize Cuddy's talk, or they can choose a topic from another unit. Note the "Language Support" phrases above on the board and review them before students begin the activity.

DURING THE PROJECT

Divide students into groups of five, and give them 10–15 minutes to prepare the content for the presentations. Once the content of each presentation is finalized, select a student from each group to be the judge. Ask the judges to leave the room. Of the remaining four students, ask two to practice high-power poses, and two to practice low-power poses for two minutes. After students practice their poses, have the judges come back. Then have each member give the presentation to their group. After all students have presented, tell the judges to guess which did high-power poses and which did low-power poses and why. Then have presenters reveal which poses they practiced.

AFTER THE PROJECT

Lead a class discussion about the presentations and the judges' results. How many judges were right? Ask students to also talk about how they felt during their presentations.

EXPLORE MORE

Encourage students to learn from each other about body language in different cultures. Or have students go online to learn about examples of powerful body language in cultures other than their own.

ENERGY BUILDERS

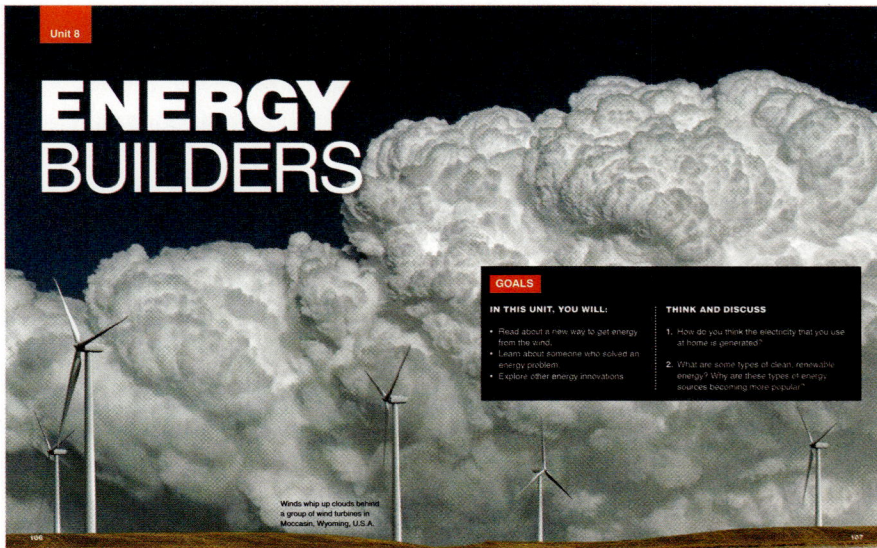

Unit 8

ENERGY BUILDERS

GOALS

IN THIS UNIT, YOU WILL:

• Read about a new way to get energy from the wind.
• Learn about someone who solved an energy problem.
• Explore other energy innovations

THINK AND DISCUSS

1. How do you think the electricity that you use at home is generated?

2. What are some types of clean, renewable energy? Why are these types of energy sources becoming more popular?

Winds whip up clouds behind a group of wind turbines in Moccasin, Wyoming, U.S.A.

UNIT OVERVIEW

Reading: Students are introduced to a new way to harness wind energy: the energy kite.

TED Talk: William Kamkwamba tells the story of how as a young boy he taught himself how to build a windmill, which helped his family and community survive a famine.

Project: Students watch a TED Talk about renewable energy and summarize the main points for their classmates.

Lesson 8A KITE POWER

LESSON OVERVIEW

Aims:
• Read and comprehend an article that explains why energy kites are a better alternative to traditional wind turbines.
• Scan for specific information.
• Make comparisons.

Target Vocabulary: altitudes, consistent, generate, practical, source, surface, traditional, visible

Reading Passage Summary: Students read about an important new invention in renewable energy, the energy kite. While wind power has become an increasingly significant source of renewable energy, wind turbines are expensive, require a lot of materials to build, and are only useful in a small number of places around the world. Inventor Saul Griffith's low-cost energy kite offers an alternative way to harness wind power. The light kites are lifted high up in the air to where there are stronger winds, taking up less ground space and creating more energy than traditional turbines.

TEACHING NOTES

THINK AND DISCUSS

This unit focuses on renewable energy and inventions that are helping to make it easier for us to access and use cleaner sources of energy. Use the questions in **Think and Discuss** to review and provide background information on renewable energy. Right now, most electricity in the world is still generated by fossil fuels, which are not renewable sources of energy. Most major electrical plants generate energy using coal, oil, or natural gas.

PRE-READING

A. Give students a few minutes to discuss in pairs what they know about wind power. In most cases, the wind turns a turbine, which then generates electricity. Elicit what students know about wind power and wind-generated energy. Make sure students understand that it is a renewable and clean source of energy. Ask students if they think it's an easy way to create energy or not.

Think and Discuss

1. Answers will vary. To generate electricity, a heat engine converts heat to energy. The most commonly used heat engine in the world is a steam turbine. The majority of the world's heat engines get their heat source from fossil fuels such as natural gas, coal, and oil.; **2.** Renewable energy is becoming more popular because it doesn't deplete the planet's resources. Examples include solar power, wind power, geothermal power, and hydropower.

Pre-reading

A. Answers will vary. Wind is used to turn a turbine, converting kinetic energy to mechanical energy in the process. A generator in the turbine then converts the mechanical energy to electricity.

B. 1–2. Guesses will vary. Actual answers are: **1.** The energy kite is a new way to harness wind energy; **2.** It is tethered and flown high up to where winds are strong. The smaller turbines on it generate the energy.

C. The infographic explains that the kite does not have a tower, so it costs less to make and uses less material. And the tether on the kite lets it reach high altitudes and be used in many places across the globe.

Getting the Main Ideas

1. F (energy kites reach stronger winds); **2.** T; **3.** T; **4.** T; **5.** F (fewer materials)

Scanning for Specific Information

1. one; **2.** 15; **3.** 300; **4.** 1,000

Building Vocabulary

A. 1. visible; **2.** traditional; **3.** source; **4.** generate

B. 1. altitudes; **2.** consistent; **3.** surface; **4.** practical

Making Comparisons

1. blades, shaft; **2.** tether; **3.** altitude

Getting Meaning from Context

1. b; **2.** a

Critical Thinking

1. Answers will vary. Possibilities include: Companies that create traditional turbines and countries that have invested in using them; pilots with low-flying planes **2.** Answers will vary.

B. Give students one minute to look at the picture and brainstorm some ideas together.

C. Have students check their answers to Exercise B as they look over the infographic on page 110. Ask them to comment on how close their predictions were. Then elicit explanations about the difference between traditional turbines and energy kites.

DEVELOPING READING SKILLS

GETTING THE MAIN IDEAS

Have students read the entire passage, either silently or while listening to the narrated passage on the audio. Have them work individually to complete the activity before checking answers in pairs. Point out that they should correct each false statement.

SCANNING FOR SPECIFIC INFORMATION

Remind students that we use the reading skill of scanning when we need to find specific information, such as names or statistics. Point out that for the exercise, students should use the units in the

questions to find the correct numbers in the passage. Give students only 30–45 seconds to work individually to quickly scan the text and find the answers. Check answers as a class. Note that the information for question 4 also appears in the infographic; however, it is in meters instead of feet. Students will have to scan the passage to find the correct answers in feet.

BUILDING VOCABULARY

A. Have students complete Exercise A individually before checking answers as a class. The word *source* can refer to a person, place, or thing where something originally comes from. A person who is a *source* may be someone who told you some gossip, or gave you some advice. News reporters routinely refer to people who give them information as a *source*. If that source does not want to be named, they are an *anonymous source*.

B. Have students complete Exercise B individually before checking answers as a class. Make sure students know to use the noun *altitude* when talking about great heights, such as mountains and airplanes in flight. Otherwise, we use the word *height*. For example, we would use *height* NOT *altitude* to talk about how tall we are. Note that *altitudes* is used in plural when talking in general about great heights.

MAKING COMPARISONS

Have students work individually to complete the activity before checking answers in pairs. Go over the language used in each sentence. Ask if the sentence is comparing or contrasting. For question 1, *Both . . . and . . . have* is used to compare. For questions 2 and 3, the language is used to contrast. Question 2 uses *but* to offer the contrast, while question 3 uses a comparative adjective (one with the suffix *-er*) and *than* to show contrast. If necessary, use a diagram or illustrations in the student book to point out examples of a *shaft* and *blade*.

GETTING MEANING FROM CONTEXT

Give students 30 seconds to look back and find the words in paragraph 5. Have them work individually to complete the activity before checking answers as a class. Note that some verb + preposition combinations are easier to infer than others. Students can probably infer the meaning of *made of* by looking only at the

words, but for *takes up*, they will need to look at context, or how it's used in a sentence.

CRITICAL THINKING

1. Evaluating. Have students discuss in pairs before sharing their thoughts with the class. Note that the passage gives a number of reasons why energy kites are a more efficient solution.

2. Reflecting. If necessary, give students five minutes to go online and search for information about wind power where they live. Or ask students to simply answer based on their own experiences: Do they live in a windy place or not? Ask students to discuss together and to also think of any other places they've been to with strong winds.

EXPLORE MORE

Students can hear the story of the development of the energy kite and watch it in motion in the video that Griffith shows during his TED Talk. Have students watch his talk while completing a TED Talk summary worksheet (see page 9 of this Teacher's Guide).

Lesson 8B · HOW I HARNESSED THE WIND

LESSON OVERVIEW

Aims:

- Watch and understand a talk by a young individual who built a wind turbine to help his family and community survive a famine.
- Understand causes and effects.
- Visualize a process.

TED Talk Summary: In his TED Talk, William Kamkwamba shares how he set out at age 13 to build a wind turbine. Kamkwamba's family and community in Malawi were suffering during a famine, so he decided to go to the library to learn how he could help. When he read that a wind turbine could help provide irrigation, he taught himself to build one using scrap pieces. The success of his invention not only helped his family and community survive a deadly famine, it helped expand his life, got him back in school, and led him to speak at TED not once, but twice. An annotated transcript for the edited TED Talk is on pages 74–75 of this Teacher's Guide.

TEACHING NOTES

The paragraphs and questions introduce Kamkwamba and the dire situation he and his family were facing when a famine hit Malawi in 2001. Note that the information in the second paragraph talks about how Kamkwamba's invention helped his family and community. In the TED Talk, he also talks about how he was motivated to make it to help himself get back to school. Students will look at this personal motivation in more depth in Part 1.

PART 1

PREVIEWING

Give students a minute to read the paragraph carefully. Have them work individually to guess the missing words before comparing answers in pairs. Ask students to explain their guesses to their partners. If necessary, explain that *secondary school* means high school. Play the video to have students check their answers. Elicit a quick class discussion on students'

1. Malawi; **2.** a terrible famine; **3.** He helped his family grow more food. He also helped his community.

PART 1

Previewing

Guesses will vary. Actual answers are: **1.** drop out of; **2.** receive; **3.** read; **4.** learn

Recognizing Main Points

1. He wanted to save his family from starvation, and he wanted to return to school; **2.** He went to the library to study.

Understanding Causes and Effects

d, b, f, e, a, c

Critical Thinking

Answers will vary. He is explaining why he is giving a second speech on the same topic. He is also making himself relatable to many Africans in rural areas by explaining that even as a poor farmer with limited English skills, he was still able to have an impact on

others. He is also trying to give others hope with his success story.

PART 2

Previewing

A. 1. He read that it could be used for irrigation and to generate electricity; **2.** Answers will vary. He says in his talk that he used an old bicycle, a tractor fan, pipes, and a shock absorber.

Visualizing a Process

A. In the scrap yard: bicycle frame and dynamo, tractor fan, PVC pipes, copper wire, switch; **In the fields:** tree branches

B. 5, 1, 4, 2, 3

Critical Thinking

Answers will vary. Possibilities include: Both inventions helped people in a deadly situation. Kamkwamba worked alone to make his invention, while Chen worked with a team. Both made affordable inventions, and both succeeded in saving people's lives.

guesses and the actual answers. If students got the answer incorrect, did they use a synonym with a similar meaning? *Extension:* Have pairs work together to go back to each sentence and find another word or phrase that might also work to complete it.

RECOGNIZING MAIN POINTS

Have students work individually to complete the activity before checking answers as a class. Note that for question 1 there are two possible sets of answers here because Kamkwamba talks about two motivations. First, he wanted to help his family survive the famine. He didn't want his six sisters or parents to die. The other motivation he talks about is his desire to return to school. He wanted to be able to afford the school fees so he could continue his education again. The first step for solving both problems was to go to the library to learn more. He wanted to find a way to help his family and get back to school as soon as possible.

UNDERSTANDING CAUSES AND EFFECTS

In addition to understanding cause and effect, students will also recognize the sequence of events that occur in Kamkwamba's story by completing the activity. Have them work individually before checking answers in pairs.

CRITICAL THINKING

Inferring. Students should be able to infer that Kamkwamba is a little embarrassed about his first TED Talk. He wanted to express himself better but got nervous in front of the big crowd. However, he also uses the story of his first TED Talk to show how even someone from a poor country with limited English skills can still do something that impresses many people and helps change lives.

PART 2

PREVIEWING

A. Have students work individually to answer the questions before comparing and discussing answers in pairs. For question 2, ask students to think about what they know about Kamkwamba's situation as they are making their predictions. What kind of materials could a poor farmer in Malawi have access to?

B. Play the video. Have students check their answers as they watch. Ask students to comment on their predictions, as well as what surprised them that they heard in the video.

VISUALIZING A PROCESS

A. Have students work individually to complete Exercise A before checking answers in pairs.

B. Have students work individually to complete Exercise B before checking answers as a class. Point out that there is a cause-and-effect relationship in each point of the process as well. Elicit that relationship for each step.

CRITICAL THINKING

If necessary, give students time to go back to Unit 3 to review Jane Chen and her invention. Tell them to think about how to express their ideas using the language for comparing and contrasting that they learned in Lesson A. Give students time to think about their answer to the question before leading a class discussion.

EXPLORE MORE

Ask students to talk about how Kamkwamba's presentation style improved between his two TED talks. *Extension:* Have students work in pairs to make a comparison between Kamkwamba's first and second TED Talks. Tell them to use the language they learned in Lesson A to compare and contrast.

Project | # RESEARCHING SOLUTIONS TO ENERGY PROBLEMS

PROJECT OVERVIEW:

Aims:
- Students work in pairs to research another new solution involving renewable energy.
- Students watch a TED Talk and present a summary using diagrams, photos, and video.
- Students debate which innovator is the most interesting.

Summary: Students research and teach their classmates about more innovative solutions for using renewable energy sources. Students present to other pairs about an invention or a solution they learned about in a new TED Talk. Then groups discuss which TED speaker had the most interesting story and why.

Materials: computer, Internet access, presentation software

Language Support: Agreeing or Disagreeing: *I think . . . ; In my opinion, . . . ; I agree because . . . ; I disagree. I think . . .*

TEACHING NOTES

PREPARATION

Have students watch each TED Talk while completing a TED Talk summary worksheet (see page 9 of this Teacher's Guide). Note that the instructions tell students to watch each talk before deciding which one to present about. Give students 30 minutes to do this. Then have students work in pairs to decide which talk to present on and to start to answer the questions to prepare their presentation content. Note the "Language Support" phrases above on the board and review them before students begin the activity.

DURING THE PROJECT

Monitor as pairs work together to create a presentation with diagrams, videos, photos, and more. Give assistance or feedback when necessary. Tell students they'll have two minutes to present to their groups. Divide the class into groups of three pairs. Make sure each pair is presenting on a different TED Talk. Have each present to the others. Tell those who are listening to take notes and think about which speaker they found the most interesting and why.

AFTER THE PROJECT

Tell groups to talk about each of the presentations they saw and decide whose was the most interesting. Whose presentation impressed them the most? Who had the most impressive solution? Ask students to think about how each speaker's presentation style affected the impact of their invention on the audience.

EXPLORE MORE

Remind students that they also learned about simple, low-cost inventions that changed lives in Unit 3.

Unit 9

CHANGING PERSPECTIVES

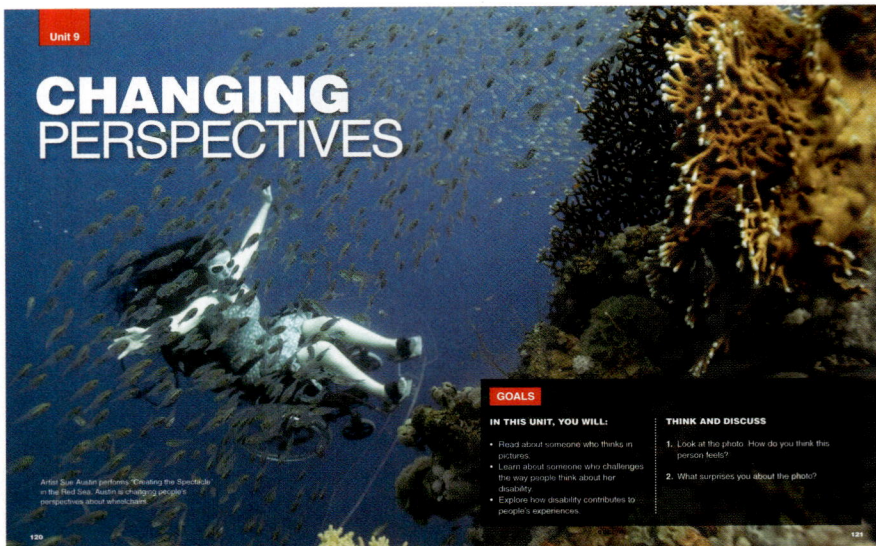

UNIT OVERVIEW

Reading: Students are introduced to a woman with autism who sees her disability as a gift.

TED Talk: Artist Sue Austin explains how her underwater wheelchair has helped change others' negative associations with wheelchairs.

Project: Students research and present about another artist challenging preconceptions about disability.

Lesson 9A   THINKING IN PICTURES

LESSON OVERVIEW

Aims:
- Read and comprehend an article about a woman with autism who has used her powers of visualization to become an animal expert.
- Scan for information and understand key details.

Target Vocabulary: affect, arrange, ignore, severe, simulation, specific, visually, welfare

Reading Passage Summary: Students read about how Temple Grandin has used her autism to become a specialist in animal behavior. Grandin is a visual thinker, meaning she thinks in images, which is the same way many animals think. She has used this talent to become an expert in designing livestock farms, and she has succeeded in creating spaces where cattle can live more peacefully. Grandin believes that the way her brain works differently has been an opportunity, not a disability, and that people with autism can help the world solve problems in new ways.

TEACHING NOTES

THINK AND DISCUSS

This unit focuses on challenging preconceptions about people with disabilities. When reviewing the goals, elicit or explain the meaning of *disability*. Ask students to look at the picture on pages 120–121. For question 1, have the class brainstorm some descriptive words that reflect what the individual in the picture may be feeling. Tell students that they will learn more about Sue Austin in the TED Talk in Lesson B. For question 2, as the class discusses what surprises them, try to gently elicit any preconceptions students might have about a person in a wheelchair.

PRE-READING

A. Give students a few minutes to discuss in pairs before leading a class discussion. Ask them to share whatever background knowledge they have about autism. As autism affects brain development, a person

Think and Discuss

1. Answers will vary. Possible answers include: happy, excited, exhilarated; **2.** Answers will vary.

Pre-reading

A. Answers will vary. See **Teaching Notes** for a detailed explanation of autism.

B. c

C. 1. Answers will vary. Animals can be unpredictable, and sometimes even dangerous. It may be hard for most people to understand how animals think and why they behave in certain ways.; **2.** Answers will vary.

Scanning for Information

1. The cause of autism is unknown; **2.** Scientists believe it begins in the early stages of brain development; **3.** Boys are four times more likely than girls to have autism; **4.** A person with autism may have delayed and disordered language, impaired social interaction, repetitive behavior, and/or a restricted range of interests.

Getting the Main Ideas

1. a; **2.** b; **3.** b

Understanding Key Details

thinks in pictures, remembers all items and visualizes them; can categorize and arrange images in a specific order; can animate images into little movies

Building Vocabulary

A. 1. affect; **2.** simulations; **3.** visually; **4.** welfare

B. 1. b; **2.** a; **3.** b; **4.** a

Getting Meaning from Context

It's a practice try or trial run to test something out before putting it to use.

Critical Thinking

1. Inferring. She means that autistic thinkers have helped solve problems that have pushed human progress forward.

2. Reflecting. Answers will vary. She presents individuals with autism as people with unique skills that are very useful, instead of as people with a disability.

---

with autism processes information differently. There are both very mild forms of autism and very severe. Characteristically, people with autism have a hard time with abstract concepts and social interactions, yet they can also excel in some fields. Students will learn in Lesson A that autism has positive aspects and can be used advantageously by an individual to make a difference.

B. Have students work individually to skim the information and complete the activity before checking answers in pairs.

C. Give students one to two minutes to think about and write their answers. Then have them discuss in pairs. Elicit some characteristics students think people who are good with animals have.

DEVELOPING READING SKILLS

SCANNING FOR INFORMATION

Have students read the entire passage, either silently or while listening to the narrated passage on the audio. Have them work individually to answer the questions.

Give them one minute to scan and complete the activity. Point out that they should use key words from the questions to scan for the information. Check answers as a class, eliciting what key words helped students find the answers quickly. Note that for question 4, there are more than three possible answers mentioned in the passage and the infographic.

GETTING THE MAIN IDEAS

At this point, students should be familiar enough with the article to understand the main ideas without looking back at the text. Have students work individually or in pairs to answer the questions before checking answers as a class.

UNDERSTANDING KEY DETAILS

Give students one to two minutes to go back to the passage and find the information. Have them work individually to complete the exercise before checking answers as a class. Note that depending how students process the information they read, answers might be slightly different. The term "thinking in pictures" may be considered a synonym for the center circle "Visual Thinking." However, some students may include it as a branch in their maps instead. Visual thinking is explained from Paragraphs 3 to 5; however, the general information that students are looking for can be found in Paragraph 3.

BUILDING VOCABULARY

A. Have students complete Exercise A individually before checking answers as a class. The noun *welfare* refers to the health, comfort, or happiness of a person or animal. It is also used to describe a social system to improve the health and happiness of people (or animals) who need help.

B. Have students complete Exercise B individually before checking answers as a class. When the adjective *severe* is used to talk about medical conditions, it means the condition is very bad. Another meaning for the adjective is "strict" or "harsh": *The punishment was severe.* In addition, it can also mean that something is very challenging: *The climb up the mountain was severe.*

GETTING MEANING FROM CONTEXT

If necessary, point out that students have learned a synonym for *test run* in the vocabulary for this unit

(simulation). A *test run* is a practice trial before the real event.

CRITICAL THINKING

Have students discuss the questions in pairs before eliciting ideas from the class. Encourage students to give reasons and examples for their opinions.

1. Inferring. Grandin believes that it's people who think differently that create progress and move us forward with new ideas and innovations.

2. Reflecting. Grandin has a very successful and happy life. Many people's stereotypes about autism come from what they've seen in movies or cases that they've heard about, which often involve individuals at the more severe end of the spectrum. Grandin provides an example of someone who has used her unique brain to offer a very positive contribution.

EXPLORE MORE

In addition to her TED Talk, students can also view a movie called *Temple Grandin* was made about Grandin. Have students find clips from the movie online. The movie trailer introduces her with the following description: innovator, author, activist, autistic.

Lesson 9B DEEP SEA DIVING . . . IN A WHEELCHAIR

LESSON OVERVIEW

Aims:
- Watch and understand a talk about how one artist is changing people's perceptions about wheelchairs.
- Understand main ideas.
- Recognize tone and message.

TED Talk Summary: In her TED Talk, artist Sue Austin shares her personal experiences of being affected by other people's perceptions of her in a wheelchair. She explains that while she felt the wheelchair was liberating, others stopped seeing her and only saw the chair. In an effort to not let this way of thinking affect her own sense of identity, she began to use art to show others how free the chair made her feel. Then she made the underwater wheelchair and began filming her adventures underwater. And with this project she felt people's perceptions really began to change. An annotated

transcript for the edited TED Talk is on pages 76–77 of this Teacher's Guide.

TEACHING NOTES

The paragraphs and questions provide background information on the TED speaker and her work. Have students work individually to read the paragraphs and answer the questions. Check answers as a class, using question 2 to encourage a discussion about preconceptions that students have of people in wheelchairs. Elicit a list of words on the board that students associate with wheelchairs.

PART 1

PREVIEWING

A. Give students a minute to read the paragraph carefully. Have them work individually to guess the

1. due to a serious illness; **2.** She felt they saw her as a person with limited mobility, and therefore didn't take time to get to know her; **3.** Answers will vary.

PART 1

Previewing

A. Guesses will vary. Actual answers are: new freedom, toy, changed, see.

B. Austin felt happy and excited to be able to move around again.

Getting the Main Idea

B. She explains that she began to believe their reactions and feel as if she really was limited and restricted by the wheelchair. The reactions began to negatively affect her perception of herself.

Critical Thinking

Inferring. She means she wanted to stop being influenced by other people's limiting views (of people in wheelchairs) and reconnect with who she really is as an individual.

PART 2

Understanding Main Ideas

A. Answers will vary.

B. 1. a; **2.** c

Recognizing Tone and Message

1. Seeing her in the chair underwater gives people a new way to view wheelchairs. They see being in a wheelchair as a valuable and different experience, not one related to limitation and loss; **2.** b, c

Critical Thinking

Comparing. Both Grandin and Austin are challenging the standard thinking that a physical or mental disability is a kind of limitation. Instead, both women show us how disabilities actually create an exciting diversity of people, which lead to new ideas and new ways of thinking. Both TED speakers show that extraordinary individuals are extraordinary individuals, no matter the circumstances.

---

missing words before comparing answers in pairs. Note that students may come up with quite a wide range of answer choices here.

B. Ask students to give reasons for their ideas in Exercise A. When partners have very different word choices, ask each to explain why they chose that word or phrase.

GETTING THE MAIN IDEA

A. Play the video to have students check their answers to **Previewing**. Ask students how accurate their guesses were. Were students surprised by any of the answers?

B. Have students work individually to answer the question before checking answers as a class. Make sure students understand what Austin means by *internalize*. She experienced people's negative impressions of her wheelchair and then started to believe them herself, even though she at first felt freed by the wheelchair. When she said it changed her on a *core level*, she means it disturbed a very deep part of her sense of identity. She began to see herself as disabled, limited, restricted. Note that this is not Austin's final response to these reactions, just her initial one. Students will hear about her final response in Part 2.

CRITICAL THINKING

Give students a few minutes to discuss their ideas with a partner. Austin clearly felt a part of her identity was taken away when she began to internalize others' negative associations about being in a wheelchair. In talking about reclaiming her identity, Austin means she felt that she had lost a part of herself because she was wrapped up in other people's stereotypes about wheelchairs. To break out of this, she had to remember and re-establish her sense of self.

PART 2

UNDERSTANDING MAIN IDEAS

A. Ask students to write down what they feel as they watch the video of Austin diving. Have students compare their answers with partners first. Did they have similar words? Then elicit students' impressions of the video. How many felt that they wanted to experience what Austin was experiencing?

B. Have students complete the questions individually before checking answers as a class. Compare students' answers to question 2 with the adjectives they wrote down in Exercise A.

RECOGNIZING TONE AND MESSAGE

Have students read and answer the questions individually. Point out that they should choose two answers for question 2. Check answers as a class. Elicit examples of word choice and language use that helped students understand Austin's tone regarding both her experience diving, as well as how it has affected others. Note that she uses words like *amazing, joy, freedom, completely new way, completely new thought, exciting new perspectives*, all of which indicate a positive tone.

CRITICAL THINKING

Give students time to think about their answer to the question. Have students discuss in pairs, giving examples from both Grandin's and Austin's stories.

EXPLORE MORE

Students can also go to wearefreewheeling.org.uk to see more examples of Austin's work.

Project

RESEARCHING PEOPLE WHO CHALLENGE OUR ASSUMPTIONS

PROJECT OVERVIEW:

Aims:
- Students work together to research unique individuals who challenge preconceptions.
- Students use maps, photos, and video to make a presentation about such an individual.
- Students discuss which person they found most interesting and why.

Summary: Students research and present on an individual who is reshaping the way people think about disabilities. Then students discuss each individual and say who they'd like to meet the most.

Materials: paper and pen or computer and printer, poster board or presentation software

Language Support: To show amazement: *Really?; Wow!; I can't believe it!; How interesting.*

TEACHING NOTES

PREPARATION

Have students work in pairs. Give them time to search online briefly for basic information about each of the people listed. Then have them choose a person to do in-depth research on. Tell them they can also choose someone else they know about who is changing preconceptions about disabilities. Ask them to find the answers to each of the questions in the student book.

Then tell them to try to find any additional interesting information to share about the person. Note the "Language Support" phrases on the board and review them before students begin the activity.

DURING THE PROJECT

Monitor as pairs work together to create a presentation with maps, videos, photos, and more. Give assistance or feedback when necessary. Tell students they'll have two minutes to present to their groups. Divide the class into groups of three or four pairs to present to the others. Make sure each pair presents on a different individual. Or have each pair present to the class. Tell those who are listening to take notes and think about which person they would most like to meet.

AFTER THE PROJECT

Tell groups to talk about each of the presentations. Ask each group member to tell the others which person they'd like to meet and why. Ask each member to also share questions that they'd like to ask that person.

EXPLORE MORE

Have students watch one or more of the TED Talks while completing a TED Talk summary worksheet (see page 9 of this Teacher's Guide). Chris Downey's talk in particular, about his experience of suddenly going blind in 2008, may be the most suitable for students of this language level.

DATA DETECTIVES

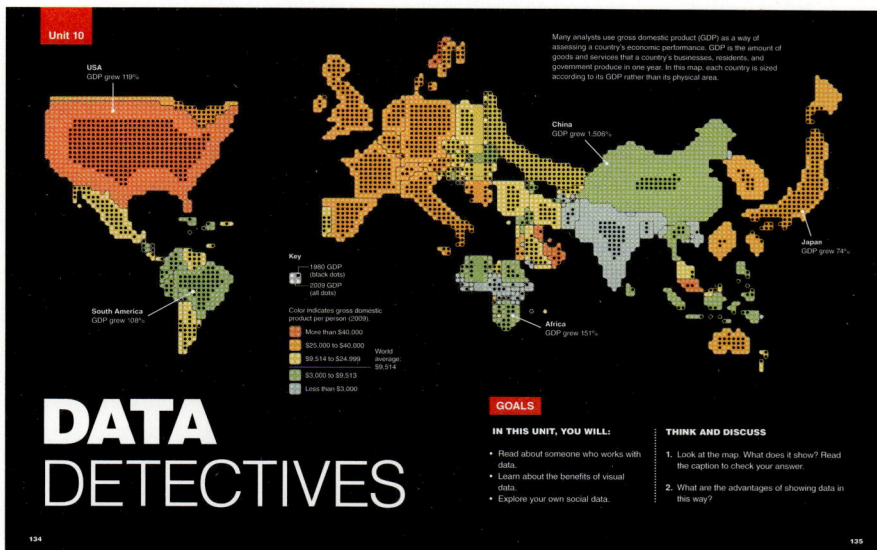

Unit 10

DATA
DETECTIVES

134   135

UNIT OVERVIEW

Reading: Students are introduced to the work and ideas of David McCandless, a journalist who designs infographics to help us better understand connections and patterns in data.

TED Talk: McCandless shares some of his infographics and explains how visual data can help us deal with the information overload.

Project: Students design an infographic to introduce to the class.

Lesson 10A INFORMATION IS BEAUTIFUL

LESSON OVERVIEW

Aims:
- Read and comprehend an article about how infographics have the power to change the way we see the world.
- Understand main idea and details.
- Understand infographics.

Target Vocabulary: appreciate, complex, connections, consume, create, enhancing, magical, visualizing

Reading Passage Summary: Students read about how infographics can help us process information more effectively and efficiently. Infographic designer David McCandless talks about how and why visuals can help us make sense of the information overload we experience in modern times. Not only do good infographics help us understand our world better, they can give us a new perspective on it.

TEACHING NOTES

THINK AND DISCUSS

Give students a minute to look over the map before checking answers as a class. While most maps show the size of countries based on land mass, this one represents size based on GDP. If necessary, elicit the meaning of *GDP*. Note that it is explained in the text on the infographic. Ask students if the visualization of the information makes it easier for them to understand it, and why or why not.

PRE-READING

A. Give students one to two minutes to look over the infographic on pages 136–137 and write their answers individually, before discussing with a partner. Note for item 4, while the infographic shows which ice sheets are getting smaller, it does not show *why* they are getting smaller.

B. Have students work individually to write their answers before discussing with a partner. Ask students to try to see the overall message and main

Think and Discuss

1. The map shows GDP, and its growth, by country; **2.** Answers will vary. For some, seeing data and information visually helps them understand it more quickly.

Pre-reading

A. The following should be checked: 1, 2, 3

B. It shows how and when rising sea levels, due to the melting of ice sheets, will cover major world cities.

C. Answers may vary, but most will likely agree that the infographic is interesting and accurate while offering an attractive design that's easy to read.

D. Answers will vary. McCandless explains that the hidden connections, patterns, and stories in information is what makes it beautiful. This is what he tries to show in his infographics.

Getting the Main Ideas

1. b; **2.** b

Understanding Details

A 1. 3, 4, 5, 7

B. Answers will vary.

C. a. data from various sources;

b. connections, patterns, and stories within data; **c.** interesting and useful infographics

Understanding Infographics

1. The size represents the country's GDP relative to others, while the color shows the average GPD per person in that country; **2.** The black dots show the size of the GDP in 1980, while all the dots (light and dark) show the GDP in 2009; **3.** c; **4.** The map and the dots are the graphic representations of the information, while the key and the notes on the map help explain it.

Getting Meaning from Context

A. "Data glut" refers to the overwhelming amount of data accessible to us today; **B.** information overload (the first line of Paragraph 4)

Building Vocabulary

A. 1. b; **2.** c; **3.** a; **4.** a

B. created; visualize; connection; appreciate

Critical Thinking

1. Since we read so much of the information we take in, an infographic gives our eyes and brain a break, and a new way of looking at things.

2. Answers will vary.

---

ideas of the infographic in the same way they do when reading a passage. Check answers as a class. Note that global warming is not mentioned at all on the infographic, yet can be inferred as an important part of the story.

C. Have students work in pairs to look over the infographic about information design on page 138. Students should note that a good infographic contains the following four points: interest, function, form, and integrity. Each point is explained in more detail on the infographic. For example, *function* refers to easiness, usefulness, usability, fit. Note that *form* may be a subjective matter for students—some may like the look of the infographic while others do not.

D. Have students work individually or discuss in pairs before checking answers. McCandless says that the hidden connections, patterns, and stories that exist in information is what makes it beautiful.

DEVELOPING READING SKILLS

GETTING THE MAIN IDEAS

Have students read the entire passage, either silently or while listening to the narrated passage on the audio. Have them answer the questions individually before checking answers in pairs. Ask students whether they agree with this and how they experience it in their own lives.

UNDERSTANDING DETAILS

A. Have students work individually or in pairs to complete the activity. Give them enough time to refer back to the passage. Point out that the four items should appear in the passage and focus on why infographics are useful.

B. Check answers to Exercise A, going over each item and eliciting why it's a reason for the usefulness of infographics or not.

C. Have students work individually to complete the statements before checking answers in pairs.

UNDERSTANDING INFOGRAPHICS

Point out that students should use the infographic on the **Think and Discuss** page to answer Exercise A. Give students a few minutes to work individually. Have students check answers in pairs before discussing question 4.

GETTING MEANING FROM CONTEXT

Have students work alone to answer both questions before checking answers in pairs. Then elicit or explain the meaning of *glut*. When there is a glut of something, there is too much of it. The word is often used to refer to a supply of goods, and synonyms include *surplus* and *excess*. Students should be able to understand from the passage that *data glut* means the same as *information overload*.

BUILDING VOCABULARY

A. Have students complete Exercise A individually before checking answers as a class.

B. Have students complete Exercise B individually before checking answers as a class. To *appreciate* something means to value and see the worth of it. In this case, the verb *appreciate* is used to talk about people, things, or experiences that we value.

CRITICAL THINKING

1. Inferring. Give students a minute to think about their answers before discussing in pairs. Check answers as a class. Point out that McCandless, who is fond of visuals, is using a visual image to help us understand his point about infographics.

2. Personalizing. Give students five to ten minutes to gather the information and complete the infographic before sharing it with a partner.

EXPLORE MORE

Note that the title of each infographic on the site pops up when the infographic is scrolled over. Many of the infographics on McCandless's site are interactive. He speaks about interactive infographics in his TED Talk.

Lesson 10B # THE BEAUTY OF DATA VISUALIZATION

LESSON OVERVIEW

Aims:
- Watch and understand a talk about infographics and how they can change the way we perceive the world.
- Understand main ideas and key details.

TED Talk Summary: In his TED Talk, McCandless engages the audience by sharing examples of his infographics, while commenting on the benefits of seeing information visually. He calls data the new soil, meaning that it is fertile ground for us to grow new ideas. The connections and patterns that emerge from the data that McCandless has gathered and put in an infographic give people a beautiful way to learn new and interesting things about the world. He explains that it's about asking the right question amidst all the information out there. An annotated transcript for the edited TED Talk is on pages 78–79 of this Teacher's Guide.

TEACHING NOTES

The paragraph tells us more about McCandless's background, and how he started making infographics even though he has no formal training in design. It builds on the information students already learned about McCandless and his work in Lesson A.

PART 1

PREVIEWING

A. Elicit the meaning of the word *break-up*. Have students work individually to complete Exercise A. Then have them check answers in pairs and discuss.

B. Give students a minute to read the paragraph carefully. Have them work individually to guess the missing words before comparing answers in pairs. Note that students may come up with quite a wide range of answer choices.

1. He does not have formal training in design or in computer graphics; **2.** Both a journalist and an infographic designer have to research and gather information, and then convey the information to others in a meaningful way; **3.** He had looked at many visuals during his research as a journalist, which gave him a basic understanding of good design.

PART 1

Previewing

A. A "break-up" refers to the end of a romantic relationship. There are likely easier times to break up with someone, such as before Spring Break, than others, like Christmas Day.

B. Guesses will vary. Actual answers are: look, numbers, patterns.

Getting the Main Idea

1. They took data from 10,000 Facebook status updates about break-ups.

2. He says they ask the right kinds of questions and work the data in the right kind of way. He means that he asks specific questions to find connections and patterns that focus his data search.

Critical Thinking

1. Answers will vary.

2. Data is like oil because it is something humans have come to depend on and to mine. Data is like soil because it provides a platform from which to cultivate and grow interesting ideas. We are sowing this "soil" by finding the connections, patterns, and stories in it that McCandless talks about.

PART 2

Understanding Main Ideas

b

Understanding Key Details

A. 1. F (more); **2.** F (many studies); **3.** T; **4.** T

B. 1. d; **2.** b; **3.** a; **4.** c

Critical Thinking

1. Answers will vary. He means that the information can change our thinking because it can show us a more well-rounded and representative picture by helping us see connections and patterns that we might not otherwise have noticed.

2. Answers will vary.

GETTING THE MAIN IDEA

Have students read the questions. Explain that they should check their answers to Exercise B of **Previewing** as well as listen for their answer to the questions while watching Part 1 of McCandless's talk. Then play the video. Ask students to comment on their answers to Exercise B first. For question 2, ask students to share their ideas about what it means to "ask the right kind of questions or work it in the right kind of way." If necessary, explain that McCandless is talking about knowing how to use data to find connections and patterns, and answers to the questions you have.

CRITICAL THINKING

1. Reflecting. Give students a few minutes to think and write their ideas individually first. Note that data is most likely taken from the United States, so the data could be very different from students' home countries. Additionally, it's important to note that people who talk about their break-ups on social media (where

McCandless got this data) on the very day the break-up happened, may not have been in very serious relationships to begin with.

2. Analyzing. Give students a few minutes to discuss in pairs first. Then elicit a class discussion. The metaphor of oil contains the idea that there is an abundance of data and it has money-making value, but it needs to be utilized in a way other than its raw form. The metaphor of soil contains the idea that data is a rich source that we can use to grow things, to connect things, and to enrich our wel-being. Humans "mine" oil, while we "sow" soil.

PART 2

UNDERSTANDING MAIN IDEAS

Have students work individually to complete the activity before checking answers as a class.

Ask students to try to visualize the idea of knowledge compression in their minds. What kind of visual do they see?

UNDERSTANDING KEY DETAILS

A. Have students work individually to read the statements. Then play the video. Check answers as a class. Ask students to share their ideas about what kind of story this infographic is telling. Note that the term *snake oil* refers to bogus medicine, something that doesn't actually help the ailment that it promises to. By titling this infographic "Snake Oil," McCandless is communicating that he is trying to find out which supplements have real, proven benefits and which don't.

B. Have students work individually to complete the activity. Have students check answers in pairs. Then ask them to summarize in their own words what McCandless is saying.

CRITICAL THINKING

1. Interpreting. Give students time to think about their answers to the question. Have students discuss in pairs, giving reasons for their answers. Make sure students understand the wordplay in the quote: The similarity in the word choice (dataset, a group of related data, and mindset, an attitude or way of thinking) helps make the point more interesting and impactful.

2. Reflecting. Have students discuss in pairs. Ask students to give examples and reasons for their opinions.

EXPLORE MORE

Students can also go to informationisbeautiful.net to study McCandless's infographics in more detail.

Project | CREATING AN INFOGRAPHIC

PROJECT OVERVIEW:

Aims:
- Students work together to design an infographic and present it to others.
- Students analyze and evaluate each other's ideas and offer feedback.

Summary: Students create an infographic based on data they find in the student book or online. They synthesize the data and present the important points visually, trying to use the four elements of a good infographic that they learned about in the unit. Pairs then present and explain their infographics.

Materials: paper, pen, colored pens, poster board

Language Support: Presentation language: *Today, I am going to introduce . . . ; Let me first explain . . . ; Let's next talk about . . .*

TEACHING NOTES

PREPARATION

Have students work in pairs. Encourage them to look through the entire student book and find a topic of interest. Or let them go online to gather data. Note the "Language Support" phrases above on the board, and review them before students begin the activity.

DURING THE PROJECT

As students research, ask them to focus on the most important information. Tell pairs to discuss how they think this information will be best presented. Encourage students to get inspiration from some of the infographics in the unit. Monitor as pairs work together on their infographics. Give assistance or feedback when necessary. Give teams two minutes to practice their presentations before showing the class their infographic and explaining it. Remind students to take notes while listening to each other's presentations and think of any questions or comments they might have.

AFTER THE PROJECT

Ask the class to discuss each of the infographics presented. Guide the discussion using the four points in Lesson A that students learned about: interest, function, form, integrity. Have students go back to the infographic on page 138 to review each point as they evaluate the infographics of their classmates. Then have the class vote on the best infographic.

EXPLORE MORE

Aaron Koblin uses huge amounts of data to create art. Students can also see examples of his work on aaronkoblin.com.

TEDTALK ANNOTATED VIDEO TRANSCRIPTS

How to Start a Movement

Part 1

So, **ladies and gentlemen**[1], at TED we talk a lot about leadership and how to make a movement. So let's watch a movement happen, start to finish, in under three minutes and **dissect**[2] some lessons from it.

First, of course you know, a leader needs the **guts**[3] to stand out and be ridiculed. But what he's doing is so easy to follow. So here's his first follower with a crucial role; he's going to show everyone else how to follow.

Now, notice that the leader **embraces**[4] him as an equal. So, now it's not about the leader anymore; it's about them, plural. Now, there he is calling to his friends. Now, if you notice that the first follower is actually an underestimated form of leadership in itself. It takes guts to stand out like that. The first follower is what transforms a **lone nut**[5] into a leader.

And here comes a second follower. Now it's not a lone nut, it's not two nuts—three is a crowd, and a crowd is news. So a movement must be public. It's important to show not just the leader, but the followers, because you find that new followers emulate the followers, not the leader.

Now, here come two more people, and immediately after, three more people. Now we've got momentum. This is the tipping point. Now we've got a movement. So, notice that, as more people join in, it's less risky. So those that were sitting on the fence before, now have no reason not to. They won't stand out, they won't be ridiculed, but they will be part of **in-crowd**[6] if they hurry. So, over the next minute, you'll see all of those that prefer to stick with the crowd because eventually they would be ridiculed for not joining in. And that's how you make a movement.

Part 2

But let's **recap**[7] some lessons from this. So first, if you are the type, like the shirtless dancing guy that is standing alone, remember the importance of nurturing your first few followers as **equals**[8] so it's clearly about the movement, not you. Okay, but we might have missed the real lesson here.

The biggest lesson, if you noticed—**Did you catch it?**[9]—is that leadership is over-glorified. That, yes, it was the shirtless guy who was first, and he'll get all the credit, but it was really the first follower that transformed the lone nut into a leader. So, as we're told that we should all be leaders, that would be really ineffective.

If you really care about starting a movement, have the courage to follow and show others how to follow. And when you find a lone nut doing something great, have the guts to be the first one to stand up and join in. And what a perfect place to do that, at TED.

Thanks.

---

[1] Note that while it's mostly considered outdated now to use the *lady* or *gentlemen* as a general reference to a woman or a man, the term "ladies and gentlemen" is still a common expression used to address a large audience of both men and women.

[2] When you "dissect" something, you take it apart and analyze it piece by piece.

[3] "Guts" is a colloquial term used to describe having characteristics of confidence, bravery, and determination

[4] "To embrace someone" can mean both to hug someone or to welcome them into your group. In the video in Sivers' TED Talk, the shirtless man both physically and figuratively "embraces" his first follower.

[5] A "lone nut" is an individual seen as crazy, whose strange actions are done alone.

[6] The "in-crowd" refers to the group doing what is considered popular at the time; a group others often look up to.

[7] When we "recap" something, we review it point by point. Note that "Let's recap" is a useful term for students to use in their Project presentations when going over the main points one more time.

[8] Someone who is your "equal" is someone you consider on the same level as you—someone with the same status.

[9] The verb "catch" is used here to mean both notice and/or understand something that might not be obvious at first. The speaker asks "Did you catch it?" to draw the audience's attention to a point they might have missed.

Conserving the Canopy

Part 1

. . . I'd like to take you all on a journey up to the forest canopy, and share with you what canopy researchers are asking and also how they're communicating with other people outside of science.

Let's start our journey on the forest floor of one of my study sites in Costa Rica. Because of the overhanging leaves and branches, you'll notice that the understory is very dark, it's very **still**[1]. And what I'd like to do is take you up to the canopy, not by putting all of you into ropes and harnesses, but rather showing you a very short clip from a National Geographic film called "Heroes of the High Frontier." This was filmed in Monteverde, Costa Rica, and I think it gives us the best impression of what it's like to climb a giant strangler fig. . . .

Up in the canopy, if you were sitting next to me and you turned around from those **primary forest ecosystems**[2], you would also see scenes like this. Scenes of forest destruction, **forest harvesting, and forest fragmentation**[3], thereby making that intact **tapestry**[4] of the canopy unable to function in the marvelous ways that it has when it is not disturbed by humans.

I've also looked out on urban places like this and thought about people who are disassociated from trees in their lives. People who grew up in a place like this did not have the opportunity to climb trees and form a relationship with trees and forests, as I did when I was a young girl. This **troubles**[5] me. . . .

Part 2

In the Pacific Northwest, there's a whole industry of moss-harvesting from **old-growth forests**[6]. These mosses are taken from the forest; they're used by the floriculture industry, by florists, to make arrangements and make hanging baskets. It's a 265-million-dollar industry, and it's increasing rapidly. . . . [What] has been stripped off of these trunks in the Pacific Northwest old-growth forest is going to take decades and decades to come back. So this whole industry is unsustainable. What can I, as an ecologist, do about that?

Well, my thought was that I could learn how to grow mosses, and that way we wouldn't have to take them out of the wild. And I thought, if I had some partners that could help me with this, that would be great. And so, I thought perhaps

---

[1] Synonyms for "still" include calm, quiet, motionless.

[2] When Nadkarni refers to "primary forest ecosystems" she is talking about the rain forest.

[3] "Forest harvesting" refers to removing trees from the forest to harvest the wood, and "forest fragmentation" refers to the way in which the forest is broken up in to pieces as a result of harvesting and other means or deforestation.

[4] A "tapestry," or textile fabric with pictures on it, is used here as a metaphor to describe the way in which all parts of the forest form one important, beauitful whole.

[5] When something "troubles someone," it worries them.

[6] "Old-growth forests" refers to very old forests that for the most part have not been disturbed by human development.

incarcerated men and women—who don't have access to nature, who often have a lot of time, they often have space, and you don't need any **sharp tools**[7] to work with mosses—would be great partners. And they have become excellent partners. The best I can imagine. They were very enthusiastic.

They were incredibly enthusiastic about the work. They learned how to distinguish different species of mosses, which, to tell you the truth, is a lot more than my undergraduate students at the Evergreen College can do. And they embraced the idea that they could help develop a research design in order to grow these mosses. We've been successful as partners in figuring out which species grow the fastest, and I've just been overwhelmed with how successful this has been. Because the prison wardens were very enthusiastic about this as well, I started a science and sustainability seminar in the prisons. I brought my scientific colleagues and sustainability **practitioners**[8] into the prison. We gave talks once a month, and that actually ended up implementing some amazing sustainability projects at the prisons—organic gardens, **worm culture**[9], recycling, **water catchment**[10] and beekeeping.

. . . Given the **duress**[11] that we're feeling environmentally in these times, it is time for scientists to reach outward, and time for those outside of science to reach towards academia as well. I started my career with trying to understand the mysteries of forests with the tools of science. By making these partnerships that I described to you, I have really opened my mind and, I have to say, my heart to have a greater understanding, to make other discoveries about nature and myself.

When I look into my heart, I see trees—this is actually an image of a real heart—there are trees in our hearts, there are trees in your hearts. When we come to understand nature, we are touching the most deep, the most important parts of our self. In these partnerships, I have also learned that people tend to **compartmentalize**[12] themselves into IT people, and movie star people, and scientists, but when we share nature, when we share our perspectives about nature, we find a **common denominator**[13]. . . .

Thank you very much.

This is an edited version of Nadkarni's 2009 TED Talk. To watch the full talk, visit TED.com.

[7.] By "sharp tools," Nadkarni is refering to knives or anything that prisoners could possibly use as a dangerous weapon.

[8.] A "practitioner" is someone who is currently active in a field of work; often in science or medicine.

[9.] "Worm culture" refers to raising worms in soil.

[10.] "Water catchment" refers to collecting water from natural sources (for drinking, etc.)

[11.] "Duress" occurs when someone is forced to do something that they don't agree with.

[12.] When you "compartmentalize," you put things in categories.

[13.] "A common denominator" is something that is shared by many, something that everyone involved has in common.

A Warm Embrace that Saves Lives

Part 1

Please close your eyes, and open your hands. Now imagine what you could place in your hands: an apple, maybe your wallet. Now open your eyes. What about a life?

What you see here is a premature baby. He looks like he's resting peacefully, but in fact he's struggling to stay alive because he can't regulate his own body temperature. This baby is so tiny he doesn't have enough fat on his body to stay warm. Sadly, 20 million babies like this are born every year around the world. Four million of these babies die annually.

But the bigger problem is that the ones who do survive grow up with severe, long-term health problems. The reason is because in the first month of a baby's life, its only job is to grow. If it's battling **hypothermia[1]**, its organs can't develop normally, resulting in a range of health problems from diabetes, to heart disease, to low I.Q. Imagine: Many of these problems could be prevented if these babies were just kept warm.

That is the **primary function[2]** of an incubator. But traditional incubators require electricity and cost up to $20,000. So, you're not going to find them in rural areas of **developing countries[3]**. As a result, parents resort to local solutions like tying hot water bottles around their babies' bodies, or placing them under light bulbs like the ones you see here—methods that are both ineffective and unsafe. **I've seen this firsthand[4]** over and over again.

On one of my first trips to India, I met this young woman, Sevitha, who had just given birth to a tiny premature baby, Rani. She took her baby to the nearest village clinic, and the doctor advised her to take Rani to a city hospital so she could be placed in an incubator. But that hospital was over four hours away, and Sevitha didn't have the means to get there, so her baby died.

Inspired by this story, and dozens of other similar stories like this, my team and I realized what was needed was a local solution, something that could work without electricity, that was simple enough for a mother or a midwife to use, given that **the majority of[5]** births still take place in the home. We needed something that was portable, something that could be sterilized and reused across multiple babies, and something **ultra[6]**-low-cost compared to the $20,000 that an incubator in the U.S. costs.

---

[1] "Hypothermia" is a dangerous condition that occurs when a person's body temperature drops too low.

[2] Something's "primary function" is what it's mainly used for—what is was made to do.

[3] The term "developing countries" refers to countries that are under-developed industrially, and usually agrarian.

[4] When you say you have "seen something first hand," you are explaining that you have seen it with your own eyes. The information is not coming from another source; you have experienced it yourself and know it to be true.

[5] "The majority of" usually refers to over fifty percent.

[6] When "ultra" is used as a prefix, it means "really" or "to an extreme degree."

Part 2

So, this is what we came up with. What you see here looks nothing like an incubator. It looks like a small sleeping bag for a baby. You can open it up completely. It's waterproof. There's no seams inside so you can sterilize it very easily. But the **magic**[7] is in this pouch of wax. This is a phase-change material. It's a wax-like substance with a melting point of human body temperature, 37 degrees Celsius. You can melt this simply using hot water and then when it melts it's able to maintain one constant temperature for four to six hours at a time, after which you simply reheat the pouch. So, you then place it into this little pocket back here, and it creates a warm **micro-environment**[8] for the baby.

Looks simple, but we've **reiterated**[9] this dozens of times by going into the field to talk to doctors, moms, and clinicians to ensure that this really **meets the needs**[10] of the local communities. We plan to **launch**[11] this product in India in 2010, and the target price point will be $25, less than 0.1 percent of the cost of a traditional incubator.

Over the next five years we hope to save the lives of almost a million babies. But the longer-term social impact is a reduction in population growth. This seems **counterintuitive**[12], but turns out that as infant mortality is reduced, population sizes also decrease, because parents don't need to anticipate that their babies are going to die. We hope that the Embrace infant warmer and other simple innovations like this represent a new trend for the future of technology: simple, localized, affordable solutions that have the potential to make huge social impact.

In designing this we followed a few basic principles. We really tried to understand **the end user**[13]—in this case, people like Sevitha. We tried to understand the root of the problem rather than being biased by what already exists. And then we thought of the most simple solution we could to address this problem. In doing this, I believe we can truly bring technology to the masses. And we can save millions of lives through the simple warmth of an Embrace.

[7.] Chen uses the noun "magic" here to explain that it (the phase-change material) is really amazing, special, and unique.

[8.] Chen uses the word "micro-environment" to explain that the wrap is a like a mini habitat for the baby.

[9.] Something that is "reiterated" is said again and again.

[10.] When you "meet the needs of" someone, you provide them with what they require.

[11.] To "launch" a product means to start selling it.

[12.] Something that is "counterintuitive" goes against what seems logical.

[13.] The term "the end user" refers to the people who are going to be using a product or service.

Gaming Can Make a Better World

Part 1

. . . This picture **pretty much sums up**[1] why I think games are so essential to the future survival of the human species. Truly. This is a portrait by a photographer named Phil Toledano. He wanted to capture the emotion of gaming, so he set up a camera in front of gamers while they were playing. And this is a classic gaming emotion. Now, if you're not a gamer, you might miss some of the nuance in this photo. You probably see the sense of urgency, a little bit of fear, but intense concentration, deep, deep focus on tackling a really difficult problem.

. . . Now, unfortunately this is more of the face that we see in everyday life now as we try to tackle urgent problems. This is what I call the "I'm Not Good At Life" face, and this is actually me making it. Can you see? Yes. Good. This is actually me making the "I'm Not Good At Life" face. This is a piece of graffiti in my old neighborhood in Berkeley, California, where I did my PhD on why we're better in games than we are in real life. And this is a problem that a lot of gamers have. We feel that we are not as good in reality as we are in games.

And I don't mean just good as in successful, although that's part of it. We do achieve more in game worlds. But I also mean good as in motivated to do something that matters, inspired to collaborate and to cooperate. And when we're in game worlds I believe that many of us become the best version of ourselves, the most likely to help at a moment's notice, the most likely to **stick with**[2] a problem as long at it takes, to get up after failure and try again. And in real life, when we face failure, when we confront obstacles, we often don't feel that way. We feel overcome, we feel overwhelmed, we feel anxious, maybe depressed, frustrated, or cynical. We never have those feelings when we're playing games, they just don't exist in games.

. . . Gamers are **super**[3]-empowered, hopeful individuals. These are people who believe that they are individually capable of changing the world. And the only problem is that they believe that they are capable of changing virtual worlds and not the real world. That's the problem that I'm trying to solve.

. . . Now, I know you're asking, "How are we going to solve real world problems in games?" Well, that's what I have **devoted**[4] my work to over the past few years, at the **Institute for the Future**[5]. We have this banner in our offices in Palo Alto, and it expresses our view of how we should try to relate to the future. We do not want to try to predict the future. What we want to do is make the future. We want to imagine the **best-case scenario**[6] outcome, and then we want to empower people to make that outcome a reality. We want to imagine epic wins, and then give people the means to achieve the epic win.

---

1. To "sum up" something means to explain it succinctly and clearly. Used together with "sums up," the modifier "pretty much" means basically. The two terms are often paired together. Another typical expression is "That pretty much sums it up."

2. When you "stick with" something you stay committed to doing it.

3. "Super" is used as a modifier for adjectives to communicate a sort of exaggerated sense of "really."

4. The verb "devote" means to be wholly committed.

5. The Institute for the Future (IFTF) is an organization in California with the mission of creating an ideal future today. The organization has a global network of leaders in various fields, and aims to support various projects focused on making a better world. McGonigal is a Research Affiliate at IFTF.

6. The phrase "best-case scenario" describes a situation with the best possible outcome. The phrase "worst-case scenario" is also commonly used.

Part 2

I'm just going to very briefly show you three games that I've made that are an attempt to give people the means to create epic wins in their own futures. So, this is World Without Oil. We made this game in 2007. This is an online game in which you try to survive an oil shortage. The oil shortage is fictional, but we put enough online content out there for you to believe that it's real, and to live your real life as if we've run out of oil. So when you come to the game, you sign up, you tell us where you live, and then we give you **real-time**[7] news, videos, **data feeds**[8] that show you exactly how much oil costs, what's not available, how food supply is being affected, how transportation is being affected, if schools are closed, if there is rioting, and you have to figure out how you would live your real life as if this were true. And then we ask you to blog about it, to post videos, to post photos.

We **piloted**[9] this game with 1,700 players in 2007, and we've **tracked**[10] them for the three years since. And I can tell you that this is a transformative experience. Nobody wants to change how they live just because it's good for the world, or because we're supposed to. But if you immerse them in an epic adventure and tell them, "We've run out of oil. This is an amazing story and adventure for you to go on. Challenge yourself to see how you would survive," most of our players have kept up the habits that they learned in this game.

So, for the next world-saving game, we decided to aim higher: bigger problem than just peak oil. We did a game called Superstruct at the Institute for the Future. And the premise was a supercomputer has calculated that humans have only 23 years left on the planet. This supercomputer was called the Global Extinction Awareness System, of course. We asked people to come online almost like a **Jerry Bruckheimer**[11] movie. You know Jerry Bruckheimer movies, you form a dream team—you've got the astronaut, the scientist, the ex-convict, and they all have something to do to save the world.

But in our game, instead of just having five people on the **dream team**[12], we said, "Everybody's on the dream team, and it's your job to invent the future of energy, the future of food, the future of health, the future of security, and the future of the social safety net." We had 8,000 people play that game for eight weeks. They came up with 500 **insanely**[13] creative solutions that you can go online, if you **google**[14] Superstruct, and see.

---

7. Something that is "real-time" is happening in the present, at the exact moment you are seeing or watching it. In McGonigal's game, players get fake news updates that are relevant for them in that exact moment in the game.

8. "Data feeds" refers to updates about news and other relevant information.

9. When a product is "piloted," it is tested out on a small group before being introduced or sold to a larger market.

10. When a research study "tracks" its participants, it follows them over a certain period of time to get updates.

11. Jerry Bruckheimer is an American movie director, well known for his action-science fiction movies following a similar storyline of a threatened world saved by an unusual group of people.

12. The term "dream team" refers to a group working together, made of very talented members. In this case, "dream" is a synonym for ideal or perfect.

13. McGonigal uses "insanely" here as a modifier meaning extremely.

14. "Google" is commonly used as a verb to mean search online.

So, finally, the last game, we're launching it March third. This is a game done with the **World Bank Institute**[15]. If you complete the game you will be certified by the World Bank Institute as a Social Innovator, class of 2010. Working with universities all over sub-Saharan Africa, and we are inviting them to learn social innovation skills. We've got a graphic novel, we've got **leveling-up**[16] in skills like local insight, knowledge networking, sustainability, vision, and resourcefulness. I would like to invite all of you to please share this game with young people, anywhere in the world, particularly in developing areas, who might benefit from coming together to try to start to imagine their own **social enterprises**[17] to save the world.

So, I'm going to **wrap up**[18] now. I want to ask a question. What do you think happens next? We've got all these amazing gamers, we've got these games that are kind of pilots of what we might do, but none of them have saved the real world yet. Well, I hope that you will agree with me that gamers are a human resource that we can use to do real-world work, that games are a powerful platform for change. We have all these amazing superpowers: blissful productivity, the ability to weave a tight social fabric, this feeling of urgent optimism, and the desire for epic meaning.

I really hope that we can come together to play games that matter, to survive on this planet for another century. And that's my hope, that you will join me in making and playing games like this. When I look forward to the next decade, I know two things for sure: that we can make any future we can imagine, and we can play any games we want. So, I say: Let the world-changing games begin. Thank you.

This is an edited version of McGonigal's 2010 TED Talk. To watch the full talk, visit TED.com.

[15.] The World Bank Institute is an organization with the goal of reducing global poverty.

[16.] In gaming, "leveling-up" happens when a gamer has played enough of one game to get a new skill or weapon or get to a new level of the game. The term is also used outside of the game world to describe doing something to improve yourself or your work situation.

[17.] A "social enterprise" is a business that has the main goal of improving a problem in society.

[18.] To "wrap up" means to finish. In speeches, the term is often said before giving a final review or summary.

The Key to Success? Grit

Part 1

When I was 27 years old, I left a very demanding job in management consulting for a job that was even more demanding: teaching. I went to teach seventh graders math in the New York City public schools. And like any teacher, I made quizzes and tests. I gave out homework assignments. When the work came back, I calculated grades.

What struck me was that I.Q. was not the only difference between my best and my worst students. Some of my strongest performers did not have **stratospheric**[1] I.Q. scores. Some of my smartest kids weren't doing so well.

And that got me thinking. The kinds of things you need to learn in seventh grade math, sure, they're hard: ratios, decimals, the area of a parallelogram. But these concepts are not impossible, and I was firmly convinced that every one of my students could learn the material if they worked hard and long enough.

After several more years of teaching, I came to the conclusion that what we need in education is a much better understanding of students and learning from a motivational perspective, from a psychological perspective. In education, the one thing we know how to measure best is I.Q., but what if doing well in school and in life depends on much more than your ability to learn quickly and easily?

Part 2

So I left the classroom, and I went to graduate school to become a psychologist. I started studying kids and adults in all kinds of super challenging settings, and in every study my question was, who is successful here and why? In all those very different contexts, one characteristic emerged as a significant **predictor**[2] of success. And it wasn't **social intelligence**[3]. It wasn't good looks, physical health, and it wasn't I.Q. It was grit.

Grit is passion and perseverance for very long-term goals. Grit is having stamina. Grit is sticking with your future, **day in, day out**[4], not just for the week, not just for the month, but for years, and working really hard to make that future a reality. Grit is living life like it's a marathon, not a sprint. . . .

Every day, parents and teachers ask me, "How do I build grit in kids? What do I do to teach kids a solid **work ethic**[5]? How do I keep them motivated for the **long run**[6]?" The honest answer is, I don't know. What I do know is that talent doesn't make you gritty. Our data show very clearly that there are many talented individuals who simply do not follow through on their commitments. In fact, in our data, grit is usually unrelated or even inversely related to measures of talent.

So far, the best idea I've heard about building grit in kids is something called "growth mindset." This is an idea developed at Stanford University by **Carol Dweck**[7], and it is the belief that the ability to learn is not fixed, that it can change with your effort. Dr. Dweck has shown that when kids read and learn about the brain and how it changes and grows in response to challenge, they're much more likely to persevere when they fail, because they don't believe that failure is a permanent condition.

So growth mindset is a great idea for building grit. But we need more. And that's where I'm going to end my remarks, because that's where we are. That's the work that stands before us. We need to take our best ideas, our strongest intuitions, and we need to test them. We need to measure whether we've been successful, and we have to be willing to fail, to be wrong, to start over again with lessons learned.

In other words, we need to be gritty about getting our kids grittier.

Thank you.

This is an edited version of Duckworth's 2013 TED Talk. To watch the full talk, visit TED.com.

---

[1] We use the adjective "stratospheric" when we want to emphasize that something is very high.

[2] A "predictor" is a thing (or person) that suggests what will happen in the future.

[3] A person's "social intelligence" is based on their ability to build social relationships with others.

[4] The phrase "day in, day out" means every day.

[5] A person's "work ethic" refers to the degree of they put effort into a task.

[6] The "long run" refers to an extended period of time from now until the far off future.

[7] Carol Dweck is a professor known for her research in motivation and intelligence.

Teach Every Child About Food

Part 1

. . . OK, school. What is school? Who invented it? What's the purpose of school? School was always invented to **arm us with**[1] the tools to make us creative, do wonderful things, make us earn a living, etc., etc., etc. You know, it's been kind of in this sort of **tight box**[2] for a long, long time. **OK?**[3] But we haven't really evolved it to deal with the **health catastrophes**[4] of America, OK? School food is something that most kids— 31 million a day, actually—have twice a day, more than often, breakfast and lunch, 180 days of the year. **So you could say that school food is quite important, really, judging the circumstances**[5]. . . .

Now, the reality is, the food that your kids get every day is fast food, it's highly processed, there's not enough fresh food in there at all. You know, the amount of additives, **E numbers**[6], ingredients you wouldn't believe—there's not enough veggies at all. French fries are considered a vegetable. Pizza for breakfast. They don't even get given **crockery**[7]. Knives and forks? No, they're too dangerous. They have scissors in the classroom, but knives and forks? No. And the way I look at it is: If you don't have knives and forks in your school, you're purely endorsing, from **a state level**[8], fast food, because it's handheld. And yes, by the way, it is fast food: It's **sloppy joes**[9], it's burgers, it's wieners, it's pizzas, it's all of that stuff. Ten percent of what we spend on healthcare, as I said earlier, is on obesity, and it's going to double. We're not teaching our kids. There's no **statutory**[10] right to teach kids about food, elementary or secondary school. OK? We don't teach kids about food. Right? And this is a little clip from an elementary school, which is very common **in England**[11].

[Video] Jamie Oliver: Who knows what this is?

Child: Potatoes.

Jamie Oliver: Potato? So, you think these are potatoes? Do you know what that is? Do you know what that is?

Child: Broccoli?

JO: What about this? Our good old friend. Do you know what this is, honey?

Child: Celery.

JO: No. What do you think this is?

---

[1] When a person is "armed with something," it's purpose is to help them be prepared for something. In this case, school arms us for the future.

[2] When Oliver calls school a "tight box," he is using this metaphor to explain things related to schooling have been set and unchanging.

[3] Note that Oliver uses the question "OK?" as a tag at the end of his statements throughout his talk. He also uses "Right?"

[4] By "health catastrophes," Oliver is referring to medical problems prevalent in the US, such as diabetes, due to obesity.

[5] If we are only reading this statement, it sounds quite straightforward. However, Oliver's delivery is given with a slight tone of sarcasm during his talk, which is why the audience laughs as he says this. Either way, Oliver is saying that of course school lunches are very important.

[6] "E numbers" refers to a system of labeling that is common in Europe. The letter E followed by a number indicates when a food contains additives.

[7] "Crockery" is a synonym for dishes, plates, and cups.

[8] The term "at state level" refers to state governments, which, in the U.S., make many of the decisions regarding schools, such those about school nutrition.

[9] A "sloppy joe" is a sandwich similar to a hamburger, except the meat is kept loose instead of shaped into a paddy, and a sweet, ketchup-based sauce is mixed in.

[10] Something that is "statutory" is required, usually by law.

[11] Note that Oliver says "in England" here even though the video clip is from a school in America. He is making the point that the same scene is also very typical in England.

Child: Onion.

JO: Onion? No.

JO: Immediately you get a really clear sense of: Do the kids know anything about where food comes from?

JO: Who knows what that is?

Child: Uh, pear?

JO: What do you think this is?

Child: I don't know.

JO: If the kids don't know what stuff is, then they will never eat it.

Normal. England and America, England and America.

Guess what fixed that. Guess what fixed that: Two one-hour sessions. We've got to start teaching our kids about food in schools, period.

Part 2

I want to tell you about something that kind of **epitomizes**[12] the trouble that we're in, guys. OK? I want to talk about something so basic as milk. Every kid **has the right to**[13] milk at school. Your kids will be having milk at school, breakfast and lunch. Right? They'll be having two bottles. OK? And most kids do. But milk **ain't**[14] good enough anymore. Because someone at **the milk board**[15], right—and don't get me wrong, I support milk—but someone at the milk board probably paid a lot of money for some **geezer**[16] to work out that if you put loads of flavorings and colorings and sugar in milk, right, more kids will drink it. Yeah. . . .

For me, there ain't no need to flavor the milk. Okay? There's sugar in everything. I know **the ins and outs**[17] of those ingredients. It's in everything. Even the milk hasn't escaped the kind of modern-day problems. There's our milk. There's our carton. In that is nearly as much sugar as one of your favorite cans of **fizzy pop**[18], and they are having two a day. So, let me just show you. We've got one kid, here, having, you know, eight tablespoons of sugar a day. You know, there's your week. There's your month. And I've taken the liberty of putting in just the five years of elementary school sugar, just from milk. . . .

[12] To "epitomize something" is to offer an exact or perfect example of it.

[13] When we "have the right to something," it means it's a basic need that we morally or legally should have.

[14] The word "ain't" is a colloquial way to say "is not", "are not", and "am not". It is generally not considered correct English, however it is used widely by native speakers in various locations around the world.

[15] The "milk board" is a government agency that makes decisions about milk production and distribution in the U.S.

[16] "Geezer" is a slang term, with a negative tone, for older man.

[17] When you know "the ins and outs" of something, you know it in great detail.

[18] "Fizzy pop" is a synonym for soda.

Part 3

Obviously in schools we owe it to them to make sure those 180 days of the year, from that little precious age of four, til 18, 20, 24, whatever, they need to be cooked proper, fresh food from local growers on site. OK? There needs to be a new standard of fresh, proper food for your children. Yeah?

Under the circumstances, it's profoundly important that every single American child leaves school knowing how to cook 10 recipes that will save their life. Life skills.

That means that they can be students, young parents, and be able to sort of duck and dive around the basics of cooking, no matter what recession hits them next time. If you can cook, recession money doesn't matter. If you can cook, time doesn't matter. . . .

I know it's weird having an English person standing here before you talking about all this. All I can say is: I care. I'm a father, and I love this country, and I believe truly, actually, that if change can be made in this country, beautiful things will happen around the world. If America does it, I believe other people will follow. It's incredibly important.

When I was in Huntington, trying to get a few things to work when they weren't, I thought "If I had a magic wand, what would I do?" And I thought, "You know what? I'd just love to be put in front of some of the most amazing **movers and shakers**[19] in America." And a month later, TED phoned me up and gave me this award. I'm here. So, my wish. **Dyslexic, so I'm a bit slow**[20]. My wish is for you to help a strong, sustainable movement to educate every child about food, to inspire families to cook again, and to empower people everywhere to fight obesity.

Thank you.

This is an edited version of Oliver's 2010 TED Talk. To watch the full talk, visit TED.com.

---

[19] The term "moves and shakers" refers to powerful people in their fields, who are usually the decision-makers.

[20] Dyslexia is reading disorder that causes problems with organizing and arranging words and thoughts. In his talk, Oliver explains that he is "dyslexic" here to explain why he is taking time to find his notes for his final statement. Note that he is also using this moment to compose his emotions.

Your Body Language Shapes Who You Are

Part 1

. . . So **we're**[1] really fascinated with body language, and we're particularly interested in other people's body language. You know, we're interested in, like, you know, an awkward interaction, or a smile, or a **contemptuous**[2] glance, or maybe a very awkward wink, . . .

So **social scientists**[3] have spent a lot of time looking at the effects of our body language, or other people's body language, on judgments. And we **make sweeping judgments**[4] and inferences from body language. And those judgments can predict really meaningful life outcomes, like who we hire or promote, who we ask out on a date. . . .

So when we think of nonverbals, we think of how we judge others, how they judge us, and what the outcomes are. We tend to forget, though, the other audience that's influenced by our nonverbals, and that's ourselves. . . .

Part 2

So my main collaborator **Dana Carney, who's at Berkeley**[5], and I really wanted to know, can you fake it till you make it? Like, can you do this just for a little while and actually experience a behavioral outcome that makes you seem more powerful? So we know that our nonverbals **govern**[6] how other people think and feel about us. There's a lot of evidence. But our question really was, do our nonverbals govern how we think and feel about ourselves?. . .

So this is what we did. We decided to bring people into the **lab**[7] and run a little experiment, and these people adopted, for two minutes, either high-power poses or low-power poses, and I'm just going to show you five of the poses, although they took on only two. So here's one. A couple more. This one has been dubbed the "Wonder Woman" by the media. Here are a couple more. So you can be standing or you can be sitting. And here are the low-power poses. So you're folding up, you're making yourself small. This one is very low-power. When you're touching your neck, you're really protecting yourself. So this is what happens. They come in, they spit into a **vial**[8], we for two minutes say, "You need to do this or this." They don't look at pictures of the poses. We don't want to **prime**[9] them with a concept of power. We want them to be feeling power, right? So two minutes they do this. We then ask them, "How powerful do you feel?" on a series of items, and then we give them an opportunity to gamble, and then we take another saliva sample. That's it. That's the whole experiment.

So this is what we find. Risk tolerance, which is the gambling, what we find is that when you're in the high-power pose condition, 86 percent of you will gamble. When you're in the low-power pose condition, only 60 percent, and that's a pretty **whopping**[10] significant difference.

---

[1] When Cuddy refers to "we" in the beginning of her talk, she means the general public.

[2] A "contemptuous" glance is one in which you clearly show that you don't like the other person.

[3] A "social scientist" does research about society and relationships.

[4] If you "make sweeping judgments" about something, you form an opinion about something and believe it to be true as a generalization.

[5] Dana Carney runs the Social and Nonverbal Behavior Lab at University of California, Berkeley.

[6] In this case, to "govern" something means to control it.

[7] "Lab" is short for "laboratory," where science experiments and research are conducted.

[8] A "vial" is a small glass container, usually in the shape of a cylinder.

[9] The verb "prime" means to prepare.

[10] The adjective "whopping" is an informal way to say "very large."

Here's what we find on testosterone. From their **baseline[11]** when they come in, high-power people experience about a 20-percent increase, and low-power people experience about a 10-percent decrease. So again, two minutes, and you get these changes. Here's what you get on cortisol. High-power people experience about a 25-percent decrease, and the low-power people experience about a 15-percent increase.

So two minutes lead to these hormonal changes that configure your brain to basically be either assertive, confident, and comfortable, or really stress-reactive, and, you know, feeling sort of **shut down[12]**. And we've all had the feeling, right? So it seems that our nonverbals do govern how we think and feel about ourselves, so it's not just others, but it's also ourselves. Also, our bodies change our minds.

Part 3

. . . So when I tell people about this, that our bodies change our minds and our minds can change our behavior, and our behavior can change our outcomes, they say to me, "I don't— It feels fake." Right? So I said, "fake it till you make it." "I don't—It's not me. I don't want to get there and then still feel like a fraud. I don't want to feel like an impostor. I don't want to get there only to feel like I'm not supposed to be here." And that really **resonated[13]** with me, because I want to tell you a little story about being an impostor and feeling like I'm not supposed to be here.

When I was 19, I was in a really bad car accident. I was thrown out of a car, **rolled[14]** several times. I was thrown from the car. And I woke up in a head injury **rehab ward[15]**, and I had been **withdrawn[16]** from college, and I learned that my I.Q. had dropped by two standard deviations, which was very traumatic.

I knew my I.Q. because I had identified with being smart, and I had been called gifted as a child. So I'm taken out of college, I keep trying to go back. They say, "You're not going to finish college. Just, you know, there are other things for you to do, but that's not going to work out for you." So I really struggled with this, and I have to say, having your identity taken from you, your core identity, and for me it was being smart, having that taken from you, there's nothing that leaves you feeling more powerless than that. So I felt entirely powerless. I worked and worked and worked, and I got lucky, and worked, and got lucky, and worked.

Eventually I graduated from college. It took me four years longer than my peers, and I convinced someone, my angel advisor, Susan Fiske, to take me on, and so I ended up at Princeton, and I was like, I am not supposed to be here. I am an impostor. And the night before my first-year talk, and the first-year talk at Princeton is a 20-minute talk to 20 people. That's it. I was so afraid of being found out the next day that I called her and said, "I'm quitting." She was like, "You are not quitting, because **I took a gamble on you[17]**, and you're staying. You're going to stay, and this is what you're going to do. You are going to fake it. You're going to do every talk that you ever get asked to do. You're just going to do it and do it and do it, even if you're terrified and just paralyzed and having an **out-of-body experience[18]**, until you have this moment where you say, 'Oh my gosh, I'm doing it. Like, I have become this. I am actually doing this.'" So that's what I did. . . .

So at the end of my first year at Harvard, a student who had not talked in class the entire semester, who I had said, "Look, you've gotta participate or else you're going to fail," came into

---

[11.] A "baseline" is the starting point; in the case of Cuddy's experiment, this refers to the levels of testosterone and cortisol that participants had before starting the experiment.

[12.] When a person feels "shut down," they are psychologically unable to respond normally to a situation.

[13.] When something "resonates" with you, you agree with it, often on a deep level.

[14.] Cuddy uses the verb "rolled" to explain that the car turned over multiple times during the accident.

[15.] "Rehab" is short for rehabilitation.

[16.] To "withdraw" from school means to "drop out" or "leave permanently."

[17.] When a person "takes a gamble on" someone, they are taking the risk to support that person even though it's not clear if the person will succeed. The expression can also be used for things, such as a new business venture.

[18.] An "out-of-body experience" describes the sensation of feeling so unfamiliar with a situation that it seems like it's not you experiencing it.

my office. I really didn't know her at all. And she said, she came in totally **defeated**[19], and she said, "I'm not supposed to be here." And that was the moment for me. Because two things happened. One was that I realized, oh my gosh, I don't feel like that anymore. You know. I don't feel that anymore, but she does, and I get that feeling. And the second was, she is supposed to be here! Like, she can fake it, she can become it. So I was like, "Yes, you are! You are supposed to be here! And tomorrow you're going to fake it, you're going to make yourself powerful, and, you know, you're gonna—" "And you're going to go into the classroom, and you are going to give the best comment ever." You know? And she gave the best comment ever, and people turned around and they were like, oh my God, I didn't even notice her sitting there, you know?

She comes back to me months later, and I realized that she had not just faked it till she made it, she had actually faked it till she became it. So she had changed. And so I want to say to you, don't fake it till you make it. Fake it till you become it. . . . So I want to ask you first, you know, both to try power posing, and also I want to ask you to share the science, because this is simple. **I don't have ego involved in this**[20]. Give it away. Share it with people, because the people who can use it the most are the ones with no resources and no technology and no status and no power. Give it to them because they can do it in private. They need their bodies, privacy and two minutes, and it can significantly change the outcomes of their life.

Thank you.

This is an edited version of Cuddy's 2012 TED Talk. To watch the full talk, visit TED.com.

---

[19] A person who feels "defeated" is demoralized.

[20] When Cuddy explains "I don't have ego involved in this." she means that she doesn't need credit for her power poses; she simply wants people who can benefit from them to start using them.

How I Harnessed the Wind

Part 1

Thank you. Two years ago, I stood on the TED stage in Arusha, Tanzania. I spoke very briefly about one of my proudest creations. It was a simple machine that changed my life.

Before that time, I had never been away from my home in Malawi. I had never used a computer. I had never seen **an Internet**[1]. On the stage that day, I was so nervous. My English lost, I wanted to vomit. I had never been surrounded by so many **azungu**[2], white people.

There was a story I wouldn't tell you then. But well, I'm feeling good right now. I would like to share that story today. We have seven children in my family. All sisters, excepting me. This is me with my dad when I was a little boy. Before I discovered the wonders of science, I was just a simple farmer in a country of poor farmers. Like everyone else, we grew **maize**[3].

One year, our fortune turned very bad. In 2001 we experienced an awful famine. Within five months all Malawians began to starve to death. My family ate one meal per day, at night. Only three swallows of nsima for each one of us. The food passes through our bodies. We drop down to nothing. In Malawi, the **secondary school**[4], you have to pay school fees. Because of the hunger, I was forced to drop out of school. I looked at my father and looked at those dry fields. It was the future I couldn't accept.

I felt very happy to be at the secondary school, so I was determined to do anything possible to receive education. So I went to a library. I read books, science books, especially physics. I couldn't read English that well. I used diagrams and pictures to learn the words around them.

Part 2

Another book put that knowledge in my hands. It said a windmill could pump water and generate electricity. Pump water meant irrigation, **a defense against**[5] hunger, which we were experiencing by that time. So I decided I would build one windmill for myself. But I didn't have materials to use, so I went to a **scrap yard**[6] where I found my materials. Many people, including my mother, said I was crazy.

I found a tractor fan, shock absorber, PVC pipes. Using a bicycle frame and an old bicycle **dynamo**[7], I built my machine. It was one light at first. And then four lights, with switches, and even a circuit breaker, modeled after an electric bell. Another machine pumps water for irrigation.

Queues[8] of people start lining up at my house to charge their mobile phone. I could not **get rid of**[9] them. And the reporters came too, which lead to bloggers and which lead to a call from something called TED. I had never seen an airplane before. I had never slept in a hotel. So, on stage that day in Arusha, my English lost, I said something like, "I tried. And I made it."

So I would like to say something to all the people out there like me to the Africans, and the poor who are struggling with your dreams. **God bless**[10]. Maybe one day you will watch this on the Internet. I say to you, trust yourself and believe. Whatever happens, don't give up. Thank you.

---

[1] As Kamkwamba is not a native English speaker, his speech at times contains some errors typical of non-native learners. Note that instead of "an," the article "the" should be used when referring to "the Internet."

[2] Kamkwamba's native language is Chichewa. "Azungu" is a word from this language.

[3] "Maize" is another way to say "corn".

[4] "Secondary school" is a typical way to say "high school" in British English.

[5] Something that is "a defense against" aims to protect others from a threatening situation.

[6] A "scrap yard" is a place where garbage that can't be easily disposed of is kept.

[7] A "dynamo" is a machine that turns mechanical energy into electric energy.

[8] The word "queue" is used in British English for "line (of people)."

[9] When you try to "get rid of" someone, you try to make them leave.

[10] The expression "God Bless," while religious in nature, is usually said in a general way to offer someone good wishes.

Deep Sea Diving . . . In a Wheelchair

Part 1

. . . I started using a wheelchair 16 years ago when **an extended illness¹** changed the way I could access the world. When I started using the wheelchair, it was a tremendous new freedom. I'd seen my life **slip away²** and become restricted. It was like having an enormous new toy. I could **whiz around³** and feel the wind in my face again. Just being out on the street was exhilarating.

But even though I had this newfound joy and freedom, people's reaction completely changed towards me. It was as if they couldn't see me anymore, as if an **invisibility cloak⁴** had descended. They seemed to see me in terms of their assumptions of what it must be like to be in a wheelchair. When I asked people their associations with the wheelchair, they used words like limitation, fear, pity, and restriction. I realized I'd internalized these responses and it had changed who I was on a core level. A part of me had become **alienated⁵** from myself. I was seeing myself not from my perspective, but vividly and continuously from the perspective of other people's responses to me.

As a result, I knew I needed to make my own stories about this experience, new narratives to reclaim my identity.

Part 2

I started making work that aimed to communicate something of the joy and freedom I felt when using a wheelchair—a power chair—to **negotiate⁶** the world. I was working to transform these internalized responses, to transform the preconceptions that had so shaped my identity when I started using a wheelchair, by creating unexpected images. The wheelchair became an object to paint and play with. When I literally started leaving traces of my joy and freedom, it was exciting to see the interested and surprised responses from people. It seemed to open up new perspectives, and therein lay the **paradigm shift⁷**. It showed that an arts practice can remake one's identity and transform preconceptions by revisioning the familiar.

So when I began to dive, in 2005, I realized scuba gear extends your range of activity in just the same way as a wheelchair does, but the associations attached to scuba gear are ones of excitement and adventure, completely different to people's responses to the wheelchair.

So I thought, "I wonder what'll happen if I put the two together?" [Laughter] And the underwater wheelchair that has resulted has taken me on the most amazing journey over the last seven years.

So to give you an idea of what that's like, I'd like to share with you one of the outcomes from creating this spectacle, and show you what an amazing journey it's taken me on. . . .

It is the most amazing experience, beyond most other things I've experienced in life. I literally have the freedom to move in 360 degrees of space and an ecstatic experience of joy and freedom.

And the incredibly unexpected thing is that other people seem to see and feel that too. Their eyes literally light up, and they

---

¹· The expression "an extended illness" is often used to refer to a serious illness that lasted a long time.

²· When something "slips away," it slowly disappears.

³· To "whiz around" means to move quickly through the air; it is often used to talk about going quickly on a vehicle with wheels, such as a bicycle, motor bike, or wheelchair.

⁴· The term "invisibility cloak," refers to a magical cape that makes you invisible. The term is best known for being used in the Harry Potter series by British author J.K. Rowling.

⁵· Someone who is "alienated" is isolated or feels alone.

⁶· When we speak about "negotiating" in reference to a place or space, the verb means to move through or over that space, often with special effort. It is often used to talk about overcoming an obstacle, but can also be used generally, as in this case ("the world").

⁷· When "a paradigm shift" occurs, people start thinking in a completely new way.

say things like, "I want one of those," or, "If you can do that, I can do anything."

And I'm thinking, it's because in that moment of them seeing an object they have no **frame of reference**[8] for, or so transcends the frames of reference they have with the wheelchair, they have to think in a completely new way. And I think that moment of completely new thought perhaps creates a freedom that spreads to the rest of other people's lives. For me, this means that they're seeing the value of difference, the joy it brings when instead of focusing on loss or limitation, we see and discover the power and joy of seeing the world from exciting new perspectives. For me, the wheelchair becomes a vehicle for transformation. In fact, I now call the underwater wheelchair "Portal," because it's literally pushed me through into a new way of being, into new dimensions and into a new level of consciousness.

And the other thing is, that because nobody's seen or heard of an underwater wheelchair before, and creating this **spectacle**[9] is about creating new ways of seeing, being and knowing, now you have this concept in your mind. You're all part of the artwork too.

This is an edited version of Austin's 2012 TED Talk. To watch the full talk, visit TED.com.

---

[8] A "frame of reference" is a set of ideas or assumptions that we use when forming preconceptions about something.

[9] The noun "spectacle" refers to an especially exciting display to watch.

The Beauty of Data Visualization

Part 1

. . . So, I've been working as a data journalist for about a year, and I keep hearing a phrase all the time, which is this: "Data is the new oil." Data is the kind of **ubiquitous**[1] resource that we can shape to provide new innovations and new insights, and it's all around us, and it can be **mined**[2] very easily. It's not a particularly great metaphor in these times, **especially if you live around the Gulf of Mexico**[3], but I would, perhaps, adapt this metaphor slightly, and I would say that data is the new soil. Because for me, it feels like a fertile, creative medium. Over the years, online, we've laid down a huge amount of information and data, and we irrigate it with networks and connectivity, and it's been worked and tilled by unpaid workers and governments. And, all right, I'm kind of milking the metaphor a little bit. But it's a really fertile medium, and it feels like visualizations, infographics, data visualizations, they feel like flowers blooming from this medium. But if you look at it directly, it's just a lot of numbers and disconnected facts. But if you start working with it and playing with it in a certain way, interesting things can appear and different patterns can be revealed.

Let me show you this. Can you guess what this data set is? What rises twice a year, once in Easter and then two weeks before Christmas, has a mini peak every Monday, and then flattens out over the summer? I'll take answers. [Audience: Chocolate.] David McCandless: Chocolate. You might want to get some chocolate in. Any other guesses? [Audience: Shopping.] DM: Shopping. Yeah, retail therapy might help. [Audience: Sick leave.] DM: Sick leave. Yeah, you'll definitely want to take some time off. Shall we see?

So, the information **guru**[4] Lee Byron and myself, we **scraped**[5] 10,000 **status Facebook updates**[6] for the phrase "break-up" and "broken-up" and this is the pattern we found—people clearing out for Spring Break, [Laughter] coming out of very bad weekends on a Monday, being single over the summer, and then the lowest day of the year, of course: Christmas Day. Who would do that? So there's a titanic amount of data out there now, unprecedented. But if you ask the right kind of question, or you work it in the right kind of way, interesting things can emerge. . . .

Part 2

We need relative figures that are connected to other data so that we can see a **fuller picture**[7], and then that can lead to us changing our perspective. As **Hans Rosling**[8], the master, my master, said, "Let the dataset change your mindset." And if it can do that, maybe it can also change your behavior.

Take a look at this one. I'm a bit of a health nut. I love taking supplements and being fit, but I can never understand what's going on in terms of evidence. There's always conflicting evidence. Should I take vitamin C? Should I be taking wheatgrass? This is a visualization of all the evidence for nutritional supplements. This kind of diagram is called a balloon race. So the higher up the image, the more evidence there is for each supplement. And the bubbles correspond to popularity as regards to **Google hits**[9]. So you can immediately apprehend the relationship between efficacy and popularity, but you can also, if you grade the evidence, do a "worth it" line. So supplements above this line are worth investigating, but only for the conditions listed below, and

---

[1] Something that is "ubiquitous" seems to be everywhere.

[2] In this case, "mine" means to exploit a resource.

[3] When McCandless mentions the Gulf of Mexico, he is referring to the oil spill that occurred there in the spring of 2010. McCandless's talk was given in July of the same year.

[4] A "guru" is an expert on and teacher of a specific topic.

[5] In computer terminology, to "scrape" means to copy data using a program.

[6] The "status Facebook updates" that McCandless used in his research are posts that individuals made on their social networking profile pages.

[7] The expression "fuller picture" refers to seeing the whole situation, instead of only a specific part of it. A similar expression is "the big picture."

[8] Hans Rosling is a statistics expert from Sweden and a TED speaker. Like McCandless, he is well known for using infographics in his work.

[9] "Google hits" refers to the list of results when a term is put into in the search engine Google.

then the supplements below the line are perhaps not worth investigating.

Now this image constitutes a huge amount of work. We scraped like 1,000 studies from PubMed, the biomedical database, and we compiled them and graded them all. And it was incredibly frustrating for me because I had a book of 250 visualizations to do for **my book**[10], and I spent a month doing this, and I only filled two pages. But what it points to is that visualizing information like this is a form of knowledge compression. It's a way of squeezing an enormous amount of information and understanding into a small space. And once you've **curated**[11] that data, and once you've cleaned that data, and once it's there, you can do cool stuff like this.

So I converted this into an interactive app, so I can now generate this application online—this is the visualization online—and I can say, "Yeah, brilliant." So it **spawns**[12] itself. And then I can say, "Well, just show me the stuff that affects heart health." So let's filter that out. So heart is filtered out, so I can see if I'm curious about that. I think, "No, no. I don't want

to take any synthetics, I just want to see plants and—just show me herbs and plants. I've got all the natural ingredients." Now this app is spawning itself from the data. The data is all stored in a Google Doc, and it's literally generating itself from that data. So the data is now alive; this is a living image, and I can update it in a second. New evidence comes out. I just change a row on a spreadsheet. **Doosh!**[13] Again, the image recreates itself. So it's cool. It's kind of living. . . .

So, just to **wrap up**[14], I wanted to say that it feels to me that design is about solving problems and providing elegant solutions, and information design is about solving information problems. It feels like we have a lot of information problems in our society at the moment, from the overload and the saturation to the breakdown of trust and reliability and runaway skepticism and lack of transparency, or even just interestingness. I mean, I find information just too interesting. It has a magnetic quality that draws me in. . . .

This is an edited version of McCandless's 2010 TED Talk. To watch the full talk, visit TED.com.

[10.] When he talks about "my book," McCandless is likely referring to a book called *The Visual Miscellaneum* which McCandless authored in 2009. He has since published two other books of his infographics, *Information is Beautiful* and *Knowledge is Beautiful.*

[11.] To "curate" data means to choose it and organize it.

[12.] To "spawn" means to produce or generate something. McCandless uses this term twice in his talk to explain how an interactive infographic re-creates itself when a user specifies which data to include.

[13.] The word "Doosh!" that McCandless uses here works as a kind of sound effect. While it is not a widely used expression, McCandless uses "Doosh!" a few times in his full-length TED talk to create a sense of drama when showing his infographics.

[14.] Note that McCandless uses the same term that McGonigal did in Unit 5 when finishing the talk: "wrap up."

Image Credits

10 ©AFP/Getty Images. **15** ©Rob Nelson. **20** ©Ami Vitale/Ripple Effect Images. **25** ©FREDERIC J. BROWN/Getty Images. **30** ©James P. Blair/National Geographic Creative. **35** ©Edwin Remsberg/VWPics/Redux. **40** ©Richard Heathcote/Getty Images, Sport/Getty Images. **45** ©Paul Richman/500px Prime. **50** ©RED/Freewheeling/Norman Lomax. **55** ©John Tomanio, NGM Staff. Cartogram: XNR Productions and John Tomanio. Sources: World Bank, CIA World Fact Book, Econstats (Cartogram); UN (Population Graphic); Oxford Forecasting (GDP Graphic); U.S. Energy Information Agency (Energy Graphic; OECD is the Organization for Economic Cooperation and Development).

Acknowledgements

The Authors and Publisher would like to thank the following teaching professionals for their valuable input during the development of this series:

Coleeta Paradise Abdullah, Certified Training Center; **Wilder Yesid Escobar Almeciga,** Universidad El Bosque; **Tara Amelia Arntsen,** Northern State University; **Mei-ho Chiu,** Soochow University; **Amy Cook,** Bowling Green State University; **Anthony Sean D'Amico,** SDH Institute; **Mariel Doyenart,** Alianza Cultural Uruguay-Estados Unidos; **Raichle Farrelly,** American University of Armenia; **Douglas E. Forster,** Japan Women's University; **Rosario Giraldez,** Alianza Cultural Uruguay-Estados Unidos; **Floyd H. Graham III,** Kansai Gaidai University; **Jay Klaphake,** Kyoto University of Foreign Studies; **Anthony G. Lavigne,** Kansai Gaidai University; **Adriana Castañeda Londoño,** Centro Colombo Americano; **Alexandra Dylan Lowe,** SUNY Westchester Community College; **Elizabeth Ortiz Lozada,** COPEI - COPOL English Institute; **David Matijasevich,** Canadian Education College; **Jennie Popp,** Universidad Andrés Bello; **Ubon Pun-ubon,** Sripatum University; **Yoko Sakurai,** Aichi University; **Michael J. Sexton,** PSB Academy; **Jenay Seymour,** Hongik University; **Karenne Sylvester,** New College Manchester; **Mark S. Turnoy; Hajime Uematsu,** Hirosaki University; **Nae-Dong Yang,** National Taiwan University;